It looks like summer has finally arrived—I've been cramped up in this apartment working on this book for too long! I realize now that we never finished our conversation about the Spanish Civil War: that revolutionary moment when anarchists came so close to actually creating a new society not only worth dying for but worth living for.

Our talks seemed to last forever. You filled me in on the background, the gritty details of militias and collectives, resistance and solidarity—everything. I always thought of it as "the closest we ever got," something to be admired and obsessed over. It nearly drove me crazy to imagine the possibilities they had! How could we not mythologize the struggles of far off places like Spain and fantasize what it be like to right in a *real* revolution?

I realized today, looking at the pages of this book, *that I don't give a damn about the Spanish Civil War*. Not to say that it wasn't an important moment in history, but legends alone aren't enough for me anymore. I don't think of them as the "real" anarchists compared to the "second-rate" anarchists that we see ourselves to be. We have to live and struggle against what we face today. The anarchists of revolutionary Spain would probably rather we fight our own struggles today than spend so much time discussing theirs! The Spanish anarchists were just regular folks, and they did exactly what we'll do when we get the opportunity. Our collective has been working on this book for over a year and its our broadside for anarchy today. I hope you enjoy it.

What you hold in your hands is not a traditional book. Think of it more as a DNA library or a pair of boltcutters. In other words: a *dare*. Books about "politics" usually have a concise purpose and narrowly written essays that you are expected to quickly defend or mercilessly attack. If they are successful, so we are told, the authors will win support for a particular faction or discredit a competing one. We hope for something else. We want this book to be opening up as many questions as it answers. Think of this more as a collection of field observations written by renegade anthropologists who have lit their degrees on fire to live in the forest and scale skyscrapers. Besides haunting the nation's infoshops, we have been recording the muttered prophecies of street-corner falafel vendors, writing love poetry disguised as politics, and living politics disguised as love poetry. We are anarchists who have cultivated our resistance in the heart of the American empire. This is our tiny contribution to the communities of resistance which have fed our hopes and nurtured our ambitions.

When you close a book, you're done with it. You can either entomb it upon your shelf or, if it's really something precious, give it to a friend.

Do not let this book rot on a shelf. Give it away, leave it at a vacant bus stop to be found by a stranger, or use it to keep warm on cold nights. The only way to dispose of this book is to light it on fire.

ISBN included so that we can distribute the book as widely as possible: 978-1-938660-01-6

ANARCHY

IN THE AGE OF DINOSAURS

by The Curious George Brigade

DO THE EVOLUTION!

Introduction to the Second Edition

by Strangers in a Tangled Wilderness

This book went out of print because in 2009 the US government, on a sealed warrant, stole every print copy and every digital backup from a house in New York City. The feds used authorship of the text as part of their justification for the raid in the statements they made to the media. But folk anarchy cannot be suppressed. We have no leaders to imprison, no central organization to crush. We found a secondhand copy of the book, scanned it, and laid it out for print once more.

It might be that a lot has changed in the decade since this book was written. It was published at the tail end of the anti-globalization movement, from the "summit-hopping" days when hordes of anarchists set out to put a stop to the neoliberal economic policies that were tearing the developing world asunder. Those days are behind us. Though the plunder of the world continues apace, though we continue to hold counter-summits whenever the tyrants of the world gather, we're half a decade into a global recession and nothing is the same.

The essays in this collection address some of the hot topic conversations of the milieu of their time: How do we create an inclusive, honest movement? How do we organize effectively? What's to be done with these crusty travelers? Do we do what we do for duty or for joy?

We've got a feeling that the ideas in this book will be as relevant to the new generation of anarchists as they were to the previous one. The phrase "diversity of tactics" is thrown around a lot, but what about a diversity of ideas? A diversity of strategies? A diversity of *goals*? Folk anarchy demands that we not get caught up in a pissing contest to see who can recruit the most converts, to see which ideology can attract the most unquestioning followers. Our goal isn't to sell the most party newspapers—or even copies of this book. Our goal is to live as anarchists.

This book won't tell you how to do that. No book can. But it might help—it certainly helped us. It helped us to put words to what we'd always believed: the chaos is our ally, that we're proud to be anarchists, that there's no contradiction between working on infrastructure and attacking the machinery of oppression, that we don't need to live in the shadow of the past or while away the hours waiting for the "revolutionary moment."

That anarchy can be lived, here and now.

The Age of Dinosaurs

[Editor's Note: Below are unedited entries from Dr. Errol Falkland's recent logbook. Dr. Falkland is one of the leading researchers in paleopoliticology and his recent research has been published in *Nature*, *Left Turn*, and the *New England Review of Paleopoliticology*. He and a number of his students from Ferrer University spent this summer excavating some new sites in North America. We would like to thank Dr. Falkland and his students for providing access to these previously unpublished findings.]

We found an exceptionally rich site this week in the shallows of the Appalachians in Southwest Pennsylvania. A number of specimens were found in excellent condition, including the first complete skeletal remains of *Proletarian Maximus*. *Proletarian Maximus* is undoubtedly the ancestor of numerous other smaller forms of Proletarians (e.g. *Class-asauras*, *Anarcho-commitarius*, *Syndicalicus*, and *Polyunionus*.) What is exciting about this find is that one can easily observe the politico-environmental factors that allowed such a lumbering

beast to somehow survive into the modern age. Though there has been some disagreement among researchers, there can now be little doubt that currently isolated and endangered species, such as the Wobblienators and their ilk, are directly related to this mid-19th century behemoth.

The signifying features of this animal are its immense size, its slow movement, and its propensity to stumble into quagmires. This particular specimen was no doubt slaughtered by Federal Rex. Over the past decades, a number of partial skeleton remains of Proletarian Maximus have been found, suggesting that their slow movement made them easy prey for not only Federal Rex but also Pteralpinkertons and other larger, more dangerous predators of the mid-19th and early-20th centuries.

Evolutionarily, these animals relied on larger and larger mass to protect themselves from the predatory animals of the *Capitalismaurs* genus. Their inability to adapt and reliance on face-to-face confrontations with large predators often made them easy meals for these raptorous killers. Only the smaller forms seem to have died natural deaths, apparently not considered large enough meals for the predators and left to the marginalized areas of North America such as college campuses.

Proletarian Maximus North Americanus is often confused by even seasoned paleopoliticologists as being the same animal as *Proletarian Maximus European*, or even the specialized hybrid of P*roletarian Maximus Espand of the Iberian Plains*. Taxidermic analysis (along with new fecal research) points out important differences and goes a long way to explain the stunted growth of the *North American P. Maximus*.

Instead of a Manifesto

We live in an age of dinosaurs. All around us enormous social, economic, and political behemoths lumber through destroyed environments, casting life-threatening shadows over the entire planet. There is a titanic struggle taking place in our communities as Capitalist Rex and State-asaurus struggle to gill their bellies with more resources and power while fending off the claws of competing species such as the newly savage Pterror-dactyls. The battle between these giants is terrible and rages on, but it cannot last. Evolution is against these doomed tyrants. Already their sun is dimming and the bright eyes of others gleam in the darkness, demanding something else.

Not all of these eyes are much different from the struggling reptilian overlords that currently dominate the globe. They have inspired smaller dinosaurs waiting their turn for dominion. These smaller ones are the fossilized ideologies of the Left. Despite alluring promises, they offer only a cuddlier version of the current system, such as the "socialist" governments of Western Europe. In the end they are no more liberating than the larger masters. Their talons may be smaller and their teeth not as sharp, but their appetite and methods are the same as their larger kin. They long for mass: the eternal dream of the child to be mass-ive. They believe if they can reach enough mass, through parties, organizations, and movements, then they can challenge the master dinosaurs and tear power away from them.

In the cool shadows of the night, in the treetops of forgotten forests, and in the streets of devastated cities there are still other eyes. Quick eyes and slender bodies fed on hope, eyes that gleam with the possibility of independence. These small creatures live in the periphery, in the footsteps and shadows of dinosaurs. Their ears do not respond to the call of the smaller dinosaurs who want to consume them and create "one big dinosaur" to usurp all others. These small warm-blooded creatures are many and varied, living on the discarded abundance of the world that the dinosaurs, in their arrogance, trample over. They scheme together in the shadows and dance while the exhausted giants sleep. They build and create, find new ways to live and rediscover forgotten ones, confident that the tyranny will end.

We know that this draconian reign will not last forever: Even the dinosaurs know their age must end: the meteor will surely hit. Whether by the work of the curious, warm-blooded ones or by some unknown catastrophe, the bad days of gargantuan, reptilian authority will end. The drab uniform of armored scales will be replaced with a costume of feathers, fur, and supple skin of a million hues.

This is anarchy in the age of dinosaurs.

A Dream of Mass

The fatal flaw of dinosaur thought is an insatiable desire for mass. The roots of this hysterical urge can be traced back to the smoke-choked nights of the 19th century, a long night we have not yet left. However the exact origins of this insistence on becoming a mass do not interest us; instead, we want to understand how this dinosaur thought makes its way into our present cultures of resistance, and what we can create to replace it.

The desire for mass dictates nearly everything a dinosaur does. This insatiable lust governs not only its decisions, but also its very organization. Mass organizations, even in the presentation of themselves to others (whether potential allies or the media), engage in a primitive chest puffing to feign that they are more massive than they actually are. Just as the early dinosaurs spent nearly every moment of their waking lives in search of food, the dinosaurs of the Left expend the majority of their resources and time chasing the chimera of mass: more bodies at the protest, more signatories, and more recruits.

The continued attraction of mass is no doubt a vestigial dream from the days of past revolutions. Every lonely soul selling a radical paper under the giant shadows of gleaming, capitalist billboards and under the gaze of a well-armed cop secretly daydreams of the masses storming the Bastille, the crowds raiding the Winter Palace, or the throngs marching into Havana. In these fantasies, an insignificant individual becomes magically transformed into a tsunami of historical force. The sacrifice of her individuality seems to be a token price for the chance to be part of something bigger than the forces of oppression. This dream is nurtured by the majority of the Left, including many anarchists: the metamorphosis of one small, fragile mammal into a giant, unstoppable dinosaur.

The dream of mass is kept alive by the traditional iconography of the Left: drawings of large undifferentiated crowds, bigger-than-life workers representing the growing power of the proletariat, and aerial photographs of legions of protestors filling the streets. These images are often appealing, romantic, and empowering: in short, *good propaganda*. However; no matter how appealing, we should not trick ourselves into thinking that they are real. These images are no more real, or desirable, than the slick advertisements offered to us by the cynical capitalist system.

Traditionally, anarchists have been critical of the homogeneity that comes with any mass (mass production, mass media, mass destruction), yet many of us seem powerless to resist the image of the sea of people flooding the streets singing "Solidarity Forever!" Terms like "Mass Mobilizations," "The Working Class," and "The Mass Movement" still dominate our propaganda. Dreams of usurpation and revolution have been imprinted on our vision from past struggles: we have bought a postcard from other times and want to experience it ourselves. If immediate, massive worldwide change is our only yardstick, the efforts of a small collective or affinity group will always appear doomed to fail.

Consumer society fills our heads with slogans such as "bigger is better," and "quantity over quality" and "strength in numbers." It should come as no surprise that the dream of a bigger and better mass movement is so prevalent among radicals of all stripes. But we should not forget how much creativity, vitality, and innovation has come from those who resist being assimilated. Many times it is the tiny group that scorns the mainstream that makes the most fantastic discoveries. Whether indigenous peasants in Chiapas or a gawky kid in high school, these are the folks that refuse to be another face in the crowd.

The desire to achieve mass leads to many dysfunctional behaviors and decisions. Perhaps the most insidious is the urge to water down our politics in order to gain popular support. This all-too-common tendency leads to bland, homogenous campaigns that are the political equivalents of the professionally printed signs we see at so many protests and rallies, monotonously repeating the dogma of the organizers' message. Despite the lip service paid to local struggles and campaigns, these are only useful to a dinosaur if they can be tied into (consumed by) the mass. The diversity of tactics and messages that come easily with heterogeneous groups must be smoothed out and compromised to focus an easily digested slogan, or goal. In this nightmare, our message and actions simply become means to increase registration rolls, to fill protest pens, or add signatories on calls to action: all measures of mass.

We pay for these numbers with stifled creativity and compromised goals. Ideas that would repel the media or expand a simple message beyond a slogan ("No Blood For Oil" or "Not My President") are avoided because they might provoke discussions and rifts of opinion, and thus reduce mass. The healthy internal debates, disagreements, and regional variations must be downplayed. Yet these are the very differences that make our resistance so fluid and flexible, leading to the brashest innovations.

In these sadly predictable situations, the soundbite is king. At all times, the eyes remain on the prize: size. The desires for mass and homogeneity (which go hand in hand) limit non-conformist and radical initiatives by those who want to try something different. A common complaint about creative or militant actions is that they will not play well in the media, that they will take away from our message, or that they will perhaps alienate some constituency or another: calls for conformity usually in the form of cynical chest beating for "unity" are powerfully effective tools for censoring passionate resistance from those not beholden to mass politics. What is missing in our street demonstrations and in our communities is not unity but genuine solidarity.

In securing their own goals, dinosaurs use fear as a tool. They utilize the very real dangers we face in our daily lives in our communities of resistance. Mass organizations promise us security and strength in numbers. If you are willing to have your ideas, your issues, and your initiatives consumed by the dinosaur, you will be protected in its ample belly. No doubt, many people are willing to temporarily subsume their messages and particular forms of resistance for safety. However, the promise of safety, whether backed by protest permits or a huge list of supporters, are empty. The State has a long history of immobilizing mass movements: a dinosaur's supposed strength lies in its lumbering size. All the State needs to do is whittle away at any particular movement through arrests, co-optation, tiny concessions, intimidation, and "seats at the table."

As the movement is divided into groups that can be co-opted, its strength dissipates and morale plummets. This has been proven again and again to be an effective and time-honored technique of the State to dispatch of any movement for social and political change.

There are other dreams, dreams of anarchy, that are not haunted by lumbering proto-dinosaurs. These are not dreams of "The Revolution" but of hundreds of revolutions. These include local and international forms of resistance that manage to be both inventive and militant. The monoculture of One Big Movement searching for The Revolution ignores the lived experiences of ordinary folks. Anarchists in North America are creating something else. Sometimes without even consciously knowing it, we are shedding the baggy skin of the dinosaur Left and venturing out to create wild and unpredictable resistances: a multitude of struggles, all of them meaningful, all of them interconnected.

The dreams of anarchists are the nightmares of the small-time dinosaurs: whether they take the form of Washington politicos, well-paid union officials, or party bureaucrats. Within a diverse swarm of individuals and small groups, resistance can be anywhere and anytime, everywhere, and all the time. In the few short years since the late nineties, the mixture of the anti-globalization convergences, local activism and campaigns, travelers, techies, and solidarity with international resistances has created something new in North America. We are replacing the Mass Movement with a swarm of movements where there's no need to stifle our passions, hide our creativity, or subdue our militancy. For the impatient, it will appear that we are too few and gaining only small victories. Yet once we drop pretensions to mass supremacy we can learn that smallness is not only beautiful, but also powerful.

Delusions of Control

When faced with the unbridled wildness of reality, dinosaurs fall into fevered delusions of grandeur. In fits of madness, they recreate the world in their own overblown image, bulldozing the wild and replacing it with a wasteland that reflects their own emptiness. Where there was once the incredibly complex diversity of nature, there is now the dead simplicity of asphalt and concrete.

These habits of control are deeply ingrained not only in dinosaurs, but also in everyone they come into contact with, including the most self-styled of revolutionaries. These delusions of control affect how we form relationships with other people, articulate our own thoughts, and live our own lives. If we look at American society we cannot ignore the rates of domestic violence, the brutal self-interest, and institutionalized homophobia, sexism, and racism. Just as dinosaurs destroy physical ecosystems, they replace their social

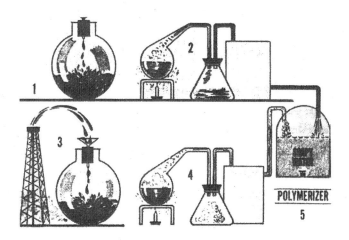

relationships with alliances and partnerships based on efficiency, control, growth, and the pursuit of profit. Anarchists have been guilty of this too. What was once a community becomes a movement; friends are replaced with mere allies. Dreams become ideology and revolution becomes work. Revolutionaries desperately attempt to control the world around them—a futile effort, since it is the twin-headed dinosaur of the State-asaurus and Multinational Business-saur that currently runs the world. Retreating from the present, radicals too often live their lives as ghosts in some revolutionary past or future. It's no surprise that revolutionaries who actually believe their own rhetoric become burnt out or, worse, armchair theorists. It's easier to ponder the future than it is to do *something* about the present.

Just as it is easier to theorize about the world than to interact with the world, it's much easier to theorize about how The Revolution will happen than to make a revolution actually happen. Predictions and postulates about which group is the most revolutionary are even more ridiculous. The theorists, being consummate experts, reserve for themselves the right to appoint the ones who will actually create revolution in the comfortably far-off future. Who are they going to choose, this time around? The workers? The proletariat?

Youth? People of color? People in the Third World? Anyone except themselves.

No one knows what The Revolution is going to look like, least of all the doddering, armchair prognosticators, who ignore their own surroundings to contemplate the perfection of the dialectic. People who stand with their feet on the ground instinctively sense that no book of revolutionary theory can capture every detail of the future. Much of what is called "revolutionary" is *irrelevant* to most ordinary folks. The voices of actual communities are alive in a way no theory could ever be even if, for now, it takes the form of tiny acts of resistance. Who doesn't cheat on taxes, avoid cops, or skip class? These acts themselves may not be revolutionary, but they begin to unravel the control from above. Anarchist approaches must be relevant to everyday experiences and flexible enough to address struggles in different situations and contexts. If we can achieve this, then we may thrive in the world after the dinosaurs. We might even be fortunate enough to be in one of the communities that have a hand in toppling them.

The State is a Machine:

Against Experts and Efficiency

Anarchists are creating a culture that allows more and more people to break free from the reign of the dinosaurs. At present, our agitation and propaganda are often just sparks to inflame the heart, not actual flames of revolution. This has provoked both impatience and cynicism in some, but anarchists should be confident. We are creating a revolution in which we don't just control the means of production, but one where we actually control our own lives.

There is no science of change. Revolution is not scientific. Activists should not be specialists in social change any more than artists should be experts in self-expression. The great lie of all experts is their claim to have access to the exclusive, the untouchable, even the unimaginable. The experts of revolution, unloved and untenured, demand many things besides your allegiance. Above all they demand efficiency—a place in the well-oiled machine.

In place of backyard gardens and public transportation, efficiency has created genetically engineered food and highways with sixteen lanes. Efficiency demands the illusion of progress no matter how meaningless. Our rejection of efficiency has led to many amazing projects. Food Not Bombs may not be the most efficient way to deliver food to those who are hungry, but they are often more effective in their aims and more meaningful than any government program, religious handout, or efficient corporation. McDonald's promises us a quick, efficient version of the dining experience; isn't that the exact opposite of what we want our world to look like? Efficiency drives many campaigns and projects; too many activists have made themselves into characters as unbelievable and shallow as those in television commercials. Their quest for efficient, marketable issues has brought them into a competition with businesses, governments, and other activists for the imagination of the public.

Like mass, efficiency is a key deity in the pantheon of dinosaur thought. There is nothing wrong with the desire to get things done; some necessary projects never hover far from drudgery and are best finished as quickly as possible. Yet our personal relationships and shared desires for change are not things to be hurried through, prerecorded, and made-for-television.

The hedged bet of the efficient activist is that since freedom is never lived but only discussed, all change must be preplanned and tedious. These experts include the bureaucrats shaking in their loafers at the thought of a folk revolt without the Party's permission or guidance. Such people have dragged their heels through revolutionary history: today they are the ones that fear the chaos of a demonstration, or talk about class struggle without reference to what is revolutionary about the refusal of constraints in daily life. Yes, they are precisely the ones with corpses in their mouths! They shiver at the thought that ideas or the people who hold them might get *out of hand.* For the self-proclaimed experts in social change, the most efficient demonstration is one with a single clear message, clear audience, and preplanned script... preferably a script written by them.

Will we ape these political machines? Will we ache to be state-like? The Leftist version of the machine will once again grind down differences to create a final product: the End of History, Utopia, The Revolution. The machines consume our vitality and contribute to the burnout so widespread in our communities. A mass mailing might be more efficient than talking to strangers, or setting up a lemonade stand in the park, but it isn't necessarily more effective. There is something to be said for taking the long route from here to there.

Any time we leave our problems to be fixed by experts, we cede a little more of our autonomy. The judges, the professors, the scientists, the politicians, the cops, the bankers: these are the engines of efficiency. Their tools can never transform our relationships   or   our society; they only calcify and harden the fucked-up ones we already have. In their world, there will always been consumers and the consumed, prisoners and captors, debtors and shareholders. The small dinosaurs who challenge the larger ones may want to change the world, but they'll do so according to a master plan written not by you or me, but by armchair experts.

The End of the Dinosaurs is Just the Beginning

There *is* a way out. The exit door out of the consumer-deathtrap-capitalist-claptrap-government-mousetrap won't be found by running away to that mythical somewhere else, whether it is a commune, the woods, or your parents' basement. We have to confront and start changing the current mess. This requires us not to act as a mass of isolated consumers following established ideologies, but as individuals creating our own futures. The old mythologies had The Revolution, Democracy, Utopia. To some extent, all of these have rung false. In the creation of something new and meaningful, we just have each other.

Our communities of resistance are scattered across North America and the world: sometimes young and furious, sometimes mature and experienced, but always ready for love or war. These interactions are the stirrings of something beautiful. Anarchists have big hearts and big dreams. We are not the first to have these thoughts: no, we have ancestors. Instead of worship or ignorance of the past, we must make our own tools, our own stories, and our own legends.

Anarchy is the name we have given to the arrow aimed at the heart of every dinosaur. It is not a religion and it is not merely an ideology or brand of politics; it is a living, evolving ecology of resistance. It is simply a promise we have made to ourselves. In the following pages you will find one collective's attempt at describing folk approaches to anarchy today. There are undoubtedly many more versions, but they are connected by a web of actions: we will fight, we will create, we will love, and we will evolve. Anarchy isn't somewhere else, some other time: *it's the most meaningful path between ourselves and freedom.*

The Next Train

"They're lazy."

"They're dirty."

"They steal and they're untrustworthy."

"They're parasites sucking up our resources."

We've all seen them. We all have an opinion about them. And most of us have let them sleep on our couches. We know all about *travelers*.

These are some common complaints anarchists settled in local communities have for their traveling brethren. When we look at these complaints, they unfortunately echo complaints from other places and other peoples. These are the same slurs and stereotypes that Eastern Europeans have against Gypsies, suburbanites have against inner city residents, unionists have against Mexican migrant workers and other immigrants, or that Germans have against Turkish guest workers.

Throughout recorded history there has been an antagonism between settled peoples and their nomadic neighbors. Part of this clash undoubtedly comes from the belief that when resources are scarce, rootless nomads will steal what settled peoples have worked for. Some argue that this tension stems from a jealousy that settled people have for people who appear to have more freedom and less constraints. Regardless of the roots of this conflict, the end result is the same: mistrust and hostility. Unfortunately many anarchists have fallen into this same trap of stereotyping and vilifying traveling folks. Yet anarchists have always traveled! Whether it was Bakunin (perhaps the original"traveling kid") organizing the First Black International, or Emma Goldman barnstorming across the US, anarchists have long taken their ideas and projects on the road. Today, we continue to take our projects and politics with us wherever and however we go: hopping trains in small groups, on bicycle extravaganzas, in cramped vans full of band equipment, on standby flights, through book tours in soccer-mom vans, or by simply sticking out our thumbs. There are several reasons to travel that exist outside of a purely hedonistic, individual realm. Travel has political and cultural potential that can strengthen our communities, cross-pollinate ideas, and provide mutual aid.

Spreading Memes

Face-to-face contact is more meaningful than communication through television, telephone, the internet, magazines, or books like this one. There is something amazing about meeting a person from another community and realizing you happen to share similar passions and projects. Travel brings us together. Now that anarchy is no longer solely the domain of dull bookfairs and college campuses, a dedicated segment of our communities has been spreading anarchist ideas across the country and world. These ideas, sometimes called "memes," mutate and change, popping up in unexpected places and contexts.

Reclaim the Streets (RTS) was originally a product of anti-road protests in Britain that were attempting to save the countryside, including the battles for Twyford Down. As more and more urban activists got involved, the scope of the protests slowly transformed from being against particular roads to being against automobile culture in general. Tripods and other tactics that have been effective at stopping the construction of roads were deployed to block already existing highways in the middle of the London. What started as standard protests became something special. Impromptu street parties complete with music, puppets, and direct action spread across England within a year; and in two years, the idea spread all the way to Finland. Within four years, the original RTS had transformed into a Global Day of Action (did you take the streets on November 30th, 1999? It was a Global Day of Action, too) with over ten thousand people in Nigeria's oil capital of Port Harcourt taking to the streets singing, dancing, and bringing to a halt the offices of the murderous oil conglomerate Shell. Mutating as it crossed the Atlantic to the United States, the RTS phenomenon has spread from the highways of London to the subway stations of New York and the suburbs of Naperville, Illinois. A substantial part of this phenomenon was transmitted by people sharing their experiences with others through their travels. The meme of RTS transcended its initial context to become meaningful for people all across the world.

Travel opens up the possibility of not only learning about people, projects, and resistances in a particular geographical community but

allows travelers to actively be involved in that community. One of the first things that travelers can offer their hosts is to do household chores (like cleaning the dishes!), but they can do much more. With her, the traveler brings knowledge, passion, and skills: a whole lifetime of experiences and accounts from other places. Without jobs and other traditional time constraints, travelers can be the cultural and political "reinforcements" for the guerilla war in which we are currently engaged in North America. Instead of being a passive recipient of information, meeting face-to-face makes us active partners in a cultural dialogue. This is the basic premise of conferences, convergences, and *encuentros*. Successful events like Louisville's Permanent Autonomous Zone (PAZ) conference brought together people from all across the country (and abroad) to share ideas, give trainings and workshops, trade patches and stencils, make contacts, and—yes—even have a good time.

In these exchanges, diversity is important: not only the racial or ethnic varieties, but also geographic. Anarchists in Kansas have their own version of anarchy which has something in common with anarchy in Maine. To various degrees, they might have something to do with Bolivian or Korean anarchy. All of these geographic communities adapt anarchist practices to their own local environment. While similarities are certainly important, the differences are where the most interesting projects spring from.

Local variation is what keeps culture alive and immediate, preventing a single vision from crowding out innovations. Like dialects of a single language, the regional variations of anarchy make us more rich and colorful. Instead of a homogenous, by-the-book ideology, anarchy has made its home in thousands of communities, based on overlapping shared cultures, politics, and practices. These different anarchies don't need to be unified, or have a uniform look. When a traveler originally from Chicago brings experiences to a temporary tree-sit encampment in the forests of Cascadia or a squatted farm in Brazil, they spread their own variation of the anarchist meme. Only time will show what happens next.

The More the Merrier

Having people come to your town from elsewhere increases morale. When anarchists swarmed to a Native American reservation in upstate New York from a half-dozen places to help protect Oneida families from being forcibly evicted from their homes, it was possible only because traveling culture is imbued with the desire to offer mutual aid. The families were surprised yet pleased at receiving help from strangers, while at the same time the anarchists were glad to become part of the community struggle, even if only temporarily. In this case, the struggle for autonomy would have been impossible without the dedication of the settled members of the community. The travelers used their "freedom" (free time and flexibility) to ensure the struggle was a success. In a rather different locale, the community gardens in the South Bronx, including the beloved Cabo Rojo, were sustained for months by travelers and anarchists from other places who built a micro-community along with their settled comrades on squatted ground. Convergences, demonstrations, and conferences have all provided the opportunities for people from different geographic communities to share and learn from each other. Traveling also has allowed groups in local struggles to expect help from unlikely allies despite geographic isolation. If a nationwide or international anarchist culture is ever to be observed, it will likely be in these sorts of interactions.

Authorities are rightly concerned by our ability to mobilize our fellows from geographic communities other than our own. In one particularly infamous Reclaim the Streets in Durham, North Carolina, the police sergeant was overheard claiming that the hundreds of anarchists there were from Eugene and San Francisco even though the protest was made up of mostly locals. The police were rightfully shocked by the participants' ability to come together successfully and do whatever they wanted. Their only explanation was somehow that the "Seattle kids" had come to menace their precinct; they were completely unaware that they had anarchists living in their own backyard. Part of the success of this particular event was that the local folks were joined by other North Carolina anarchists, college activists, street kids, and some hardy travelers. While few local communities can stage events where they are not overwhelmed by police, traveling allows us to mobilize unexpected numbers of folks and keep the authorities off balance. Instead of relying on an undifferentiated mass of people to overwhelm our enemies, we benefit from our differences and individual talents. This is the basic strength of the anti-globalization movement and is a tactic that can be useful in a variety of circumstances and struggles.

> *"Patience Makes the Hobo Strong"*
> *—graffiti in trainyard catch-out spot, Waycross,*
> *Georgia*

Borders are not only physical, they are mental. As long as we believe that we are citizens of particular countries, or limited to any single community we are losing out. We should all travel! Whether it is across the country for an IMF demonstration, or across the city to meet up with a group we've just begun a new project with, travel is a very real way to connect to other people. Our solidarity shouldn't be limited to people who happen to live in the same neighborhood or city.

Friendship is a great medium for passion: better than books, zines, or even the internet. Unfortunately many anarchists live in places far away from the scenes that will support their dreams and projects. Traveling and travelers can be a potential catalyst to allow people isolated by the chance of geography to see their projects grow and prosper without having to relocate. If anarchists ever hope to be more than a marginal force in the US, we must be able to reach even the loneliest corners of this huge country. Ironically, instead of "ruining" communities, travelers may be the best chance we have in building stronger local communities of resistance by sharing ideas, resources, and labor from different places.

Some naysayers will argue that travel is not radical, in and of itself. And this is true: a millionaire can jump on an airplane to Barbados and have an entire hotel to himself, just as a crusty in the US can ride trains motivated solely by cheap escapism. The potential of travel lies in its relative freedoms: time to dedicate to projects, the ability to convey materials and information, flexibility in putting energy into new projects, supporting faraway comrades, the list continues on. Travel can also be used to combat isolation and to give us hope in an otherwise unwelcoming world. As any traveler knows, getting somewhere you've never been requires patience and dedication: let our collective roads all lead to anarchy.

Beyond Duty and Joy

Too many friendships, collectives, and projects have been needlessly scuttled due to schisms over our basic motives for engaging in the political world. These divisions over our fundamental motivations threaten even the most ideologically "pure" projects or collectives. This obstacle is more pervasive and destructive than Green vs. Red sectarianism or the earlier division over Pacifism vs. Direct Action. They also have the unfortunate ability to rip apart friendships and leave people wondering what went wrong. Despite the perennial and pernicious aspects of this conflict over motivations, very little has been written about it from an anarchist perspective.

So what exactly is this implicit threat to collective work? The answer can be found in people's basic motivations for engaging in projects. As we all know, much of the work we do is unglamorous and demands a great deal of energy and resources. Our actions often fail to live up to our lofty expectations and at times, they can even put us in serious danger. Burnout is an incredibly common malady for activists who have put enormous amounts of time and energy into their projects. Because of these pitfalls, understanding the motivations of the people we choose to work with is every bit as important as knowing their politics. Projecting your own motivations onto others in a collective is a sure recipe for resentment and disaster.

Traditionally there have been two major strains of motivations (or perceived motivations) in anarchist politics: Duty and Joy. Like with any duality, it is easy to fall into the trap of simplistic black and white labels, ignoring the more realistic continuum of grays. It is better to think of these of two motivations as the end points on a continuum, illuminating everything in between.

Motivations cannot be separated from expectations. We are motivated to engage in particular projects because we have certain favorable expectations about our commitment. Expectations that are not collectively shared, or even expressed, can be detrimental to setting a course for projects. Because meeting expectations is the main way we evaluate the efficacy of any work or project, differences in expectations will cause differences in evaluations. These differences are capable of crippling the ability of a collective to learn from past mistakes, since different measuring sticks are being used. Just as Duty and Joy are inherently different motivations, so will there be an

equally divergent set of expectations that in turn lead to conflicting evaluations and analyses of what success means for a collective or project.

Fundamental motivational orientations, such as Duty and Joy, are more tenacious than other political disagreements because they are often a result of basic personality traits. Motivations that reside in the subconscious or unconscious are resistant to most forms intellectual arguments, historical precedents, logical manipulations, and other conscious mechanisms. In short, our reasons for doing particular projects can't always be explained intellectually. These conflicting motivational traits are potentially the most divisive element we encounter in our daily collective work. To find our way out of this minefield of motivational psychology we need to understand how these two polarizing types manifest themselves and seek new ways of doing things that complement both of them.

Duty has been the traditional motive for radical projects; until recently it was the most prevalent trend in anarchist communities. This is undoubtedly due to our tragic history. Anarchist struggles have for the most part been a string of bitter defeats, repressions, and marginalizations. So what has motivated comrades to work so hard and selflessly for so many dark years? The answer seems to be a strong sense of Duty based on a heightened notion of justice married to a belief in a better world. The Duty model has created a cult of martyrs—those who have given up everything for the Cause. Those working within the Duty model expect the work to be hard and unappreciated but still feel it must be done. Duty-bound anarchists give little thought about whether their work is joyful or fulfilling. Duty-driven political work tends to be characterized by endless meetings, struggle, shit-work, and long hours. One's commitment is measured by a simple formula of labor-hours to unpleasantness of tasks volunteered for. Sacrifice becomes a consistent and reified ideal for Duty-bound anarchists. Due to the amount of energy and unsatisfying work consumed, there is a deep concern about longevity of projects and evaluations about their effectiveness in promoting the cause. Duty tends to put a lot of emphasis on maintaining projects. Often considerable energy is used to perpetuate projects that may have outlived their original function or have never reached their potential.

The expectations of those working from a Duty model tend to be externalized. The evaluation of success and failure is based on external factors. These factors usually include media exposure, impact in the community, recruitment, funds raised, or longevity. Many of these expectations are easily quantifiable and thus empirical analysis is the prime form of evaluation for Duty-bound anarchists. This emphasis on quantity and empiricism leads to a desire to increase quantifiable results. The Duty-bound approach is similar (in motivations, expectations, and evaluations) to historic and current trends of the political Left.

Joy is a relatively new oppositional force in anarchist work, though we have always paid at least lip-service to joy in anarchist thinking. This is exemplified by Emma Goldman's famous quote "If I can't dance, I don't want to be part of your revolution." The newer joy model in anarchism comes from the punk, pagan, and traveling cultures of the late 1980s and is a direct inheritance of the hippies and 1960s New Left. Its motivation is based on the pleasure principle. Joy seeks to turn political work into play. It rejects the martyr and sacrifice tropes of the old Left and replaces them with carnival and celebratory metaphors. Joy judges political work not on labor hours or sacrifice but on how exciting and empowering a project may be on a personal and collective level. Due to the need of activism to be exciting and empowering, Joy fueled projects are often

transitory—falling apart soon after the initial thrill fades. They often give little thought to the long-term impact of projects on their community. Joy-motivated anarchists also tend to be more skeptical of the historical projects that Duty-bound anarchists revere.

Just as with Duty, activists motivated by Joy have expectations that are shaped by their motivations. The expectation of work tends to be internalized. Emphasis is given to subjective experiences and focuses on qualitative changes as opposed to quantitative measurements. Expectations often include fun, empowerment of the participants, consciousness-raising, excitement, creativity, and novelty. Projects that fail to meet these qualitative measures are viewed as deficient and ones that reach at least some of these goals as successful regardless of any outside impact. The joyful emphasis on individual needs, subjective experiences, and empowerment are more typical of certain strands of hedonistic hippie and punk subcultures than of the traditional political Left.

Since few anarchist projects neatly fit into either the Duty or the Joy styles, especially at the beginning, these personalities find themselves working together. At first, this can lead to tension and subsequently leads to resentment and expulsion. This has happened so many times in recent years that it has led to a completely irrelevant "Social Anarchism vs. Lifestyle Anarchism" debate that fails to do anything except alienate and misrepresent both types of motivations. We realize that the discussion of Duty and Joy could create a similar divide, and if this was our goal, it would be hypocritical. Instead, we should try to understand the entire spectrum of motivations without attempting to create a false "unity" in motivation, or on the other hand, starting another sectarian battle. Seeking meaning from the Duty and Joy styles can be compared to the process of achieving consensus.

A shorthand has been developed by both ends of the continuum to attack each other without shedding on light on the real motivational differences that effect their commitments. This creates yet one more way for anarchists to factionalize.

This essay is not simply a call for everyone to come together; that goal is highly unlikely and not even necessarily desirable. There are serious shortcomings in both motivational approaches (pointed out clearly by both sides of the divide) and thus a different set of

approaches is needed. To be successful a new approach must complement the strengths of both the Duty and Joy styles in order to maximize the solidarity within collectives working on anarchist projects and minimize the existing tension between people who embody either style.

The good news is that a sizable number of anarchists doing work and engaged in projects are not on either extreme of the Duty-Joy continuum. We would like to suggest a motivational approach based on Meaning. Hopefully the articulation of Meaning will not only alleviate the tension that suffocates most projects but also provide impetus for novel and successful projects.

Motivations based primarily on Meaning have always been part of anarchy; in fact, the term Meaning has been used by both the Duty and Joy camps to justify their approach while attacking each other. Since the word Meaning has been claimed by both styles, it is important to explain what is meant by motivations based on Meaning. Erich Fromm described motivations based on Meaning to "contain both the objective [Duty] and subjective [Joy] ways of understanding." Meaning is determined by analyzing the external effects and testing them against internal feelings. An anarchist motivated by Meaning seeks both personal (internalized) and public (externalized) impact from their efforts.

Projects viewed in terms of their Meaning can be evaluated more fully and appreciated more deeply from this perspective than from the other two limited approaches, namely because it acknowledges both quantifiable and qualitative desires. Our efforts can now be judged on multiple axes. No longer is it simply a matter of how many hours a person works but also of the enjoyment she can manifest from her activities. A project need not be judged simply on how exciting and fun it is but also by how effective it is in achieving its goal. Neither side of the continuum is superior to the other. Instead, harmony is sought in order to create Meaning. The application of both expectations creates a richer and more nuanced analysis of our politics. Meaning also provides a useful tool for deciding which projects are worth expending our limited energy and resources.

The Meaningful approach has the advantage of reclaiming the entire history of successful anarchist struggles and projects. It also provides a way for comrades tied to the extremes of the continuum to work with each other without surrendering or repressing their motivations. When we seek Meaning in our projects, we demand the fullest realization of our efforts and resources. We will no longer settle for either end of the continuum but seek the entire nexus.

An emphasis on Meaning limits the destructive effect of another perennial obstacle in anarchist work: burnout. Burnout comes when too much of our time and resources are squandered on meaningless projects. Meaningful endeavors actually create energy and gifts. They provide more impetus to continue our struggles, achieving longstanding projects. Meaning-based projects provide exciting opportunities and novel experiences that appeal to people all along the Duty-Joy spectrum.

In a culture that mass-produces both expectations of Duty-intensive labor and products of Joyous hedonism, Meaning justifies the price of our labor, resources, and lives. Capitalism thrives on the extremes of the Duty-Joy continuum by creating meaningless relationships that divide us into workers or consumers. Anarchy provides a solution for this absurd, dualistic society. Meaningful projects will be a better enticement for experienced anarchists and new folks alike.

Only projects that honestly attempt to balance both external and internal needs will have any hope of providing lasting resistance to the meaningless miasma of everyday consumer culture. Neither Duty nor Joy alone can develop new and better ways of living in vibrant communities of resistance. Another world is indeed possible, but it must be a meaningful one.

Butterflies, Dead Dukes, the Gypsy Wheel, and the Ministry of Strangeness

Since at least the days of Kropotkin, anarchists have consciously distanced themselves from the idea of chaos. Legends have even been whispered that the mysterious circle A represents order in chaos. Nearly every "serious" anarchist writer in recent years has tried to distance anarchism from chaos. Yet for most ordinary people, chaos and anarchy are forever linked. The connection between chaos and anarchism should be rethought and embraced, instead of being downplayed and repressed. Chaos is the nightmare of rulers, states, and capitalists. For this and other reasons, chaos is a natural ally in our struggles. We should not polish the image of anarchism by erasing chaos. Instead, we should remember that chaos is not only burning ruins but also butterfly wings.

> *"Prediction is power"*
> —*Auguste Comte, father of sociology*

Since the Enlightenment, politicians have attempted to use scientific principles in politics and economics in order to control the populace. The arrogance of sociologists, economists, and other such experts is clear in their belief that human desire can be measured, ordered, and thus controlled. The attempts to predict and control all possibilities have long been the wet dream of totalitarians and advertising executives worldwide. Since Marx, who fancied himself a "scientist of mass behavior," revolutionary vanguardists of all stripes have believed that they have discovered the perfect equation for revolution: a paint-by-numbers approach to social change. Both professional politicians and professional revolutionaries struggle to become consummate experts at manipulating the political machine; the actual politicians just happen to be better at this than their activist cousins. It's no surprise that the sociologists of revolution, earnest college Marxists, and the anarcho-literati are so enamored with platforms, policies, history, and dry theories. Unfortunately for them, and fortunately for us, chaos refuses to play by any rules.

A Little Goes A Long Way

"The flapping of a single butterfly's wing today produces a tiny change in the state of the atmosphere. Over a period of time, what the atmosphere actually does diverges from what it would have done. So, in a months time, a tornado that would have devastated the Indonesian coast doesn't happen. Or maybe one that wasn't going to happen, does."
—Edward Lorenz, meteorologist 1963

The smallest change in the initial conditions of a system can drastically change its long-term behavior. This phenomenon, common to chaos theory, is known as "sensitive dependence on initial conditions." A tiny amount of difference in a measurement might be considered experimental noise, background static, or a minor inaccuracy. Such easily dismissed changes can grow exponentially and compound in unexpected ways to create equally unexpected results far greater than anyone might imagine.

These glitches and ghosts in the machine are far too random to be predicted by any government supercomputer. Anarchists can therefore take advantage of strange turns of events, using chaos as a secret weapon against regimes of control. Who knows if a woman refusing to give up her seat on a bus will launch a Civil Rights movement, or if a tiny but angry band of kids gathering at the local hot dog stand at the right moment will set off a full-scale insurrection? Chaos can turn the tables on even the most established dinosaurs. In fluid situations such as a demonstration, seemingly inconsequential events can often shift the tone or direction of the entire "system," leading to chaos in the best possible sense of the word.

The politicians of the world hardly foresaw that the killing of Archduke Ferdinand in some backwater of the Austro-Hungarian Empire would lead to the breakup of three of the world's largest empires in less than a decade. Obviously the political tensions of the day existed independent of the dead duke, but his assassination lit a fuse whose resulting explosion destroyed the political and economic realities of empires. In the same manner; a butterfly flapping its wings at a skillshare in rural West Virginia has the potential to create a hurricane—or revolution—in Argentina.

Surfing the Fractal Waves of Revolution

Chaos is actually more real than a world easily divided into discrete objects and linear equations. These fantastical objects are too perfect to be real in anything other than a mathematics textbook. The real world is messy, feisty, and subject to constant changes beyond the grasp of any human. Abstractions can sometimes be useful when planning battles with cops, sketching out schemes for the next year, and reading maps in cities we've never been to before. Yet most abstractions do a disservice to the real world by neglecting the tiny details. The world is chaotic—and every time someone believes they can control it, the world finds yet another way to throw them off balance.

Fractal theory has shown that the real world is less "real" than we first imagined. In a much-discussed essay about the coastline of England, it was shown that the size and shape of the measuring unit dramatically affected the final outcome. If we use a straight meter stick, we will measure a shorter coastline than if we use a small curved millimeter stick. The coast of England, like it or not, is infinitely flexible. Even if you had a one-to-one map of a particular city it could never fully represent that city. There are many "cities" in any particular city and our picture of it depends on how we observe our surroundings, and what we choose to place emphasis on.

The advantage of these Borgesian realities is that anarchists have access to multiple lenses to use and understand the world. In the political realm, the authorities agree to limit themselves to one "true" representation, while we keep our eyes open to chaotic possibilities.

Anarchists can use differing perspectives and scales to determine what projects are worth working on. By the linear and grand measuring stick of Global Revolution, the details blur, and many essential projects seem less important. Revolution, like the coast of England, is influenced by what evaluating tools we use. We can utilize this flexibility in our measuring sticks to our advantage. Duty and joy are only part of the range of our motivations. Personal liberation, class war, global environmentalism, and struggles for political autonomy are all different formulas for measuring the value of an action or project. When applied to a situation, each will yield a different result.

Luck Is the Rebel's Ally

We must become allies of luck if we are to overcome the huge odds stacked against our endeavors. We cannot blithely enter the casino of political revolution and not realize the house (the status quo) is stacked against us. We can seek out luck where others have missed it. Luck is a combination of spontaneous coincidences that we can recognize and use to our advantage. These events cannot be planned or manufactured. *Luckily* for us, this complex world is filled to the brim with potentially critical coincidences that are available to any rebel intrepid enough to seek them out. This means making our plans flexible and being able to deal with these possibilities at a moment's notice. Finding a forgotten dumpster outside a parade route can easily mean the difference between getting through a police checkpoint and being thwarted, especially if that dumpster is used as a battering-ram!

How can we use chaos to our advantage in our daily resistances? When situations are unpredictable and the outcomes are unknowable, how can we hope to use such a fickle friend as an ally? These are questions for anarchist cabals and think-tanks worldwide. We can learn from every experience and not become so arrogant in thinking we can preplan every event in advance. Rigid hierarchical systems fear chaos, reject fractals, and dismiss luck. The arrogance of dinosaurs is a great advantage to our resistance. Fractalized resistance cannot be adequately met by predesigned management and crowd control strategies. It is important to realize that we are not the first ones to use chaos as a tactic. Chaos is integrated into a number of ancient and not-so-ancient cultures from the Hopi to the San bushmen. A number of communities have not only become comfortable with the inherent chaos of the world but have found effective ways to use it.

Cultures of Chaos

The nomadic Roma—also known as Gypsies—have been a "problem" for anthropologists for over a century Relatively small in number and lacking any semblance of economic, military, or political power, they have resisted assimilation for over 600 years. The Gypsies possess a fascinating and chaotic system of mutual aid based on the myth of the "Gypsy Wheel."

Material aid is freely provided to other travelers with the idea that it will be returned to the individual at some time in the future when it is needed. Only on the road (a traditionally liminal space) is mutual aid given out randomly to those who ask. This form of mutual aid is dependent on a complex and ever-shifting constellation of naturally occurring signs that outsiders believe to be quaint superstitions. Because these omens appear randomly, no individual can consciously manipulate them. Outside observers have just started to see this as a fundamental survival strategy that the Rom peoples have used against societies that wish to destroy or assimilate them. This nonlinear approach to mutual aid may appear at first too random to work for a whole society, but it has remained a supporting foundation of Rom culture. Our own interactions and generosity with strangers today often bring unexpected bounties far beyond any measurement, and *always at the right time*.

In another example from a much larger culture in a different era, for over one thousand years the Chinese empire consulted a "Ministry of Strangeness" for advice when imperial plans failed or produced unexpected results. The Ministry of Strangeness was traditionally kept in the dark about any of the original plans. The ministry would then consult the I-Ching (the random throwing and configuration of yarrow sticks) to create new plans. This effective practice was stopped when the science-orientated conqueror Genghis Khan took over. Ironically his son, Kublai Khan, reintroduced and even expanded the Ministry of Strangeness. Instead of slavishly replicating unsuccessful models and projects, we should not be afraid to try outrageous and untested schemes.

In the more specifically revolutionary realm, chaos is a tool that can knock down even the mightiest of giants. Saboteurs know that the simplest items (e.g. a wooden shoe) can be used to disrupt the most efficient and complicated systems.

Actually, the more complex a system is the easier it is to sabotage. The economic equivalent of the State's weakness to chaos is that as Capitalists become more and more dependent on technology and bureaucracy, they increase their vulnerability to chaotic forms of resistance such as hacking.

Let's acknowledge chaos as an important part of political and social change. We can integrate it as a factor into our daily lives. Chaos is the wild card that allows a small community such as ours to have an Impact much greater than expected by the experts. In fact, larger groups tend to have more inertia and rarely take advantage of the flux of the world. As long as we are not tied down to rigid tactics and brittle models, we will be able to adapt in ever-shifting environments.

With a healthy dose of suspicion towards vanguardists and experts who have the correct vision, platform, or policy for change, we can always keep our eyes open to the unexpected possibilities of chaos.

Cell, Clique, or Affinity Group?

The term "affinity group" is often bandied around in anarchist circles. However, there are quite a few misconceptions of the exact nature of affinity groups and how we can use them to bring about radical change. Affinity group structures share some obvious characteristics with both cells and cliques, yet they exist in different contexts. It can be very difficult for an outside observer to determine if any particular group of people is a cell, a clique, or an affinity group, and this has undoubtedly led to confusion. All three groups are made up of a few individuals, say three to nine, who work together, support each other, and have a structure typically closed to outsiders. Depending on their goals, they may engage in a multitude of projects, ranging from the mundane to the revolutionary, but the similarities end there.

A cell is part of a larger organization or a movement with a unified political ideology Often cells receive direction from the larger community that they are a part of. Generally, cells are "work" oriented, and do not rely on socialization as a primary goal. Particular cells are connected to one another (in the same organization) by a shared vision, though they may employ a range of tactics.

A clique, on the other hand, is a group of people who have cut themselves off from a larger community or organization. Social cliques are common; good examples can be found in any high school in groups such as jocks, preppies, geeks, or nerds. Cliques tend to be isolated and prefer to create inflexible boundaries between themselves and the rest of the community they are associated with. Cliques rarely have a focus on work or projects.

An affinity group is an autonomous group of individuals that shares a particular vision. Though the vision may not be seen identically by its members, an affinity group shares certain common values and expectations. Affinity groups emerge out of larger communities, whether they are environmentalists in a particular bioregion or members of a hip-hop group who perform together. Any two affinity groups emerging from the same community may have wildly different perspectives, interests, and tactics. This variety is uncommon amongst cells. Affinity groups maintain a stronger connection to their home communities and usually seek ways to connect to other affinity groups and organizations in that community. In this way they differ from cliques that seek to be separate. An affinity group may also work closely with other groups outside their own original community.

Affinity groups have the political advantage of being able to create connections that bridge diverse communities. Though affinity groups are mostly closed structures (a common criticism leveled by dinosaurs), most anarchists feel comfortable being part of multiple affinity groups. These personal interconnections between affinity groups can foster greater affinity and understandings between diverse communities and generate substantial solidarity. This is the "cross-pollination" effect. For example, a member of a direct action affinity group who happens to also be a member of a feminist media collective can create opportunities for both groups. The media collective may become more militant while the direct action group can be more open to feminist practices and ideas. Instead of trying to merge direct action, media, and radical feminism into an unwieldy super-group, the activist can pursue her multiple interests in two groups that put their focus on their main interest. Paradoxically, these closed affinity groups provide a safe and supportive place for broader affinities to develop, thus creating a wider web of mutual aid, understanding, and support.

While it is important to acknowledge the contextual limitations of the cell and clique models, it is a mistake to write off the affinity group for being elitist or closed. Affinity groups provide tremendous possibilities for increasing the number of connections between communities, while allowing folks a supportive environment to pursue their particular interests and affinities.

Pride, Purity, and Projects

Anarcho-pride is something worth promoting in our projects and our lives. It is a form of transparency, allowing those with whom we engage to know, in shorthand, what we believe, and how we behave. In short, it is honest. Anarcho-purity is the dark shadow of anarcho-pride. Purity demands that everyone who works together must share the same politics, agendas, and behavior—not only for a given time or project, but for the entirety of their lives. This creates a dysfunctional and unneeded strain of political Puritanism that can cripple communities and create absurd "more anarchist-than-thou" debates. These debates have ravaged the animal rights and vegan communities, not to mention dinosaur ideologies such as Christianity. The difference between pride and purity are subtle but extraordinarily important. These differences affect how we work with others and with whom we choose to spend time interacting with.

Anarcho-pride allows us to work with individuals who appreciate, if not share, our organizational principles, visions, and goals. It allows all involved to make informed decisions, whether that be putting on a benefit together or taking to the streets together. Yet many people who are anarchists are wary of broadcasting this fact to others. They fear that anarcho-pride will alienate potential allies. Unfortunately, being in the closet about our motivations is paternalistic and condescending, and can be an easy rationalization for dishonesty. Hiding our identities as anarchists presumes that other people are not intelligent or savvy enough to make the decision to work with us based on our actual politics. Political openness allows all groups to share their true goals and interests. Openness inoculates coalitions and partnerships against resentment and later misunderstandings. If groups or individuals choose to not work with us because we are anarchists, then we should respect that decision. This is better than trying to fool them into thinking we are something else and springing it on them "after the Revolution" or street action, as the case may be. Striving to create frank and open dialogue with groups and individuals we wish to work with is our best chance to foster genuine solidarity.

At the Doorstep of
Anarchist Community

Since its infancy, anarchism (like many international social movements) has been defined by its politics. No bones about it, we are political beings. Anarchists have a clear list of enemies: the State, capitalism, and hierarchy. We have an equally clear list of desires: mutual aid, autonomy, and decentralization. While we're placing bets that anarchy will provide a better life than the dinosaurs, there is little stopping anarchism from becoming yet another orthodoxy just as bad as Communism, Socialism, Liberalism, Reformism, Capitalism, Mormonism, or any other "-ism." Developments in the past several years in North America have shown that the specific tendency or narrow brand of anarchist politics are not as important as the shared communities that we are creating out of those politics. These communities are held together by practices, tactics, and culture. We don't have to be a monoculture. Instead, think of anarchy is an ecology of cultures—like microbes in the petri dish or a protest in the streets—something that demands and thrives off diversity.

Like any group of friends who work and live together, we are developing a shared culture despite our diverse origins. Every group of anarchists (including the many people who live by anarchist principles without ever opening a book by Kropotkin, Emma, or CrimethInc.) creates its own unique practices and culture. We are weary of any new orthodoxy although that is what people raised in the West are trained to desire most: the Next Big Thing, be it an author, TV show, movement, or anything other than what we're doing in our own lives. Because culture can be so fluid, transferable, and mutable, this has worked to our advantage. Instead of anarchy from above, dictated by media darlings or experts, there are dozens of competing, diverging, and mutating versions of anarchy. This is a fundamentally good development. Most anarchists are

happy with this looseness and diversity. The monoculture of dinosaurs can be rejected in favor of vibrant, folk anarchies.

Community is something that anarchists recognize and strive for. Yet what exactly these communities should be doing has been the cause of many bitter debates. Depending on who you ask it might be a pirate radio station available to a neighborhood, urban guerilla warfare, a collective house, torching ski resorts, a jazz show, or a giant demonstration. These differences lead to banal arguments that rarely aid the cultures or communities that the critics long for: instead of spending time grandstanding at the podium, we all can stand to spend more of our time creating some semblance of anarchist societies within the deranged culture we presently live in! These communities of resistance are happening throughout the world through the creation of semi-permanent autonomous zones like infoshops and community gardens, free clinics and organic farms, collective houses, and performance spaces. We see glimpses of a better world in temporary autonomous zones like mobilizations and convergences, squats and treesits, street parties and free feasts. Because creating community is hard work, our time is best spent actually manifesting and expressing our passions in these arenas, not merely talking about them.

Autonomous zones are the physical manifestations of the ideas that have grown so much in recent years, even if they appear only to be tiny storefronts, basement libraries, and warehouses scattered across North America. These are the laboratories and workshops of anarchy. As our networks expand, so has our ability to talk to each other. Our capacity to communicate has been extremely successful and prolific: music, writing, and performance. Dozens of anarchist newspapers, thousands of zines, and handfuls of books have created a media of expression and dissent. What we have today is barely a drop in the bucket compared to the capitalist media-machinery but we should not attempt to compete with them. Rejection of mass doesn't mean that anarchists are doomed to be a tiny irrelevant minority for the rest of our existence. It is possible for hundreds of thousands of collectives and affinity groups to work together in solidarity and respect for their differences.

You Can't Blow Up a Social Ecologist

Anarchy is based on the premise that leaders are neither necessary nor desirable, yet this maxim has made little impact in the authoritarian wing of the anti-authoritarian movement! Certain individuals (almost always older men with beards) develop cult followings that continue in a completely different historical context, long after their deaths. It's sad that many anarchists identify with one little clique or another, read only certain magazines, try vainly to convince everyone that their particular version of anarcho-purity is the One Right Way. These petty squabbles between factions have done far more damage to anarchy itself than any number of possible converts to their ideas could merit. If anarchists only manage to throw insults at each other over lofty theoretical issues, then of course fewer people outside the anarchist ghetto will take our ideas seriously. Anarchists should not treat each other as potential enemies and competitors for some cultural or political turf, but as potential friends and comrades in desperate need of folks with different ideas and strategies.

We aren't perfect, and just like anyone else escaping a traumatic experience such as modern Western society, most of us still carry bad habits such as dogmatism, sexism, and paternalism. A measure of mercy for ourselves would go far. The last thing our community should resemble is a political party with purges and power-plays; better we become a tribe that takes care of its own. Survival, whether in the savannas of Africa or the strip malls of the United States, means taking care of each other. Before we obsess about reaching outside organizations, or the unpoliticized masses of the working-class, or anyone beyond our anarchist communities, we should first learn to relate to each other based on solidarity, mutual aid, understanding, and respect. The empathy used when we take care of each other is the most creative tool we have to engage the rest of the world.

Intellectual nitpicking tells us these competing factions could never have a civil debate over coffee, much less work together on a practical project, right? Yet working on common projects is exactly what anarchists of different backgrounds are doing more of. We don't need unity in theory, we need solidarity in practice. Once we acknowledge and embrace our collective differences, we will be able to spread the practice of anarchy throughout our communities and the world.

Going beyond cartoon politics (put a green stripe on your black star and suddenly anarchism is reduced to saving trees; put a red stripe on your black star and anarchism is just about the class war) is absolutely vital. Sectarianism leads straight to authoritarianism, for as soon as one identifies with the correct anarcho-sect, everyone else is wrong. The founder of the correct ideology is inevitably accorded more power than his or her soon-to-be followers, and the sect musters its forces to engage in a holy war against all other brands of the anarchist rainbow. Let us not mimic the failures of other Leftists. It's much easier for us to attack each other than to destroy the State. People have different visions of liberation and any anarchist society will have a diversity of tactics and projects. Today we need radical anarchist unions capable of stopping the unceasing machine, radical writers that inspire and spread knowledge, militants to fight cops in the streets, and treesitters to save the last of wild nature: in other words, we need more anarchy!

Our Campaign Is Life

So, we want to change the world. Where to begin? A smorgasbord of issues and campaigns surrounds us on all sides, each clamoring for attention. Should we fight to save the last of the ancient forests, help the impoverished community down the street, advocate for the homeless, fight white power, combat police brutality, shut down the sweatshops, or aid the Landless Farmers' Movement in Brazil? The problems seem so much bigger than any one person or group could possibly comprehend. The world suffers from more injustice and pain than any single person could hope to heal alone. We have to do everything and more.

All around us, there is an array of ideologies offering ready-made answers, be it the latest deviant sect of communism or Hare Krishna consciousness. For those

of us who have been "changing the world" for many years, it's easy to be cynical about the supermarket of ideologies that the modern activist can buy into. We have to find some way of saving our world while avoiding easy answers and false shortcuts.

Focusing on a single campaign is a common alleyway for activists to get trapped in. Each campaign tries to advertise itself as the next crucial battle against The Man, where results will *finally* be achieved. The enemy of the particular campaign is often presented as the real master of puppets behind the ills of the world, and the enemies of all other competing campaigns nothing but puppets. Each campaign competes for members among a limited pool of activists, taking away time from not only other causes but from the daily life of the activist, leading to burn out. Every campaign wants us to buy into it—could there be a way to fight for change without treating activism as a market for justice?

Obsessive focus on single issue campaigns can lead us to treat causes, and each other, as objects with a particular value ready for display or consumption. Nearly every campaign is connected and necessary and we've got to win them all to really accomplish anything-winning in ways that the government and the corporations will never see coming. Anarchy has the flexibility to overcome many of the traditional problems of activism by focusing on revolution not as another cause but as a philosophy of living. This philosophy is as concrete as a brick being thrown through a window or flowers growing in gardens. By making our daily lives revolutionary we destroy the artificial separation between activism and everyday life. Why settle for comrades and fellow activists when we can have friends and lovers?

The Abolition of Outreach

Race is an issue that has long scared and per-
plexed radicals in the United States. White anarchists today are especially dismayed in the lack
of racial diversity especially of blacks, among the
folks who join them in the streets and collective
work. White anarchists have spent endless hours
trying to figure out "where the color is," whether
at an anti-globalization demonstration or their
local infoshop. Around the globe the majority of
anarchists are non-white. Over the last years the
anarchist community in America has started to become more like the rest of the world: ethnically
and culturally diverse. A growing number of Latinos, Asians, Arabs, and other people of color have
identified themselves as anarchists yet this does
precious little to assuage the feeling that something is missing. There can be no mistaking the fact
that what worries white anarchists the most is not
the lack of Latinos or Asians in their groups but
the lack of blacks. This may be a result of the

unique racist cultural history of the US. Race is an essential aspect of state oppression and a bulwark of exploitive capitalism. No genuine revolutionary challenge to either the State or capitalism in the United States can fail to ignore racism's importance in maintaining the current system and neither can anarchists. Unfortunately exploitive tokenism, demands for intensive outreach programs, and other failed holdovers from the Left have not made anarchist communities a welcome place for blacks.

Despite our growing racial and ethnic diversity there is still the lingering specter of an anarchist movement that is too white. White anarchists are often so frustrated by the lack of a visible presence of black folks in anarchist projects that they are easily susceptible to power plays by individuals—anarchist or not—speaking for black communities. Many times an activist (usually a white person specializing in anti-racism) has hijacked a meeting by accusing the participants of racism. Out of the fear of being labeled racist, whole collectives can be paralyzed by their inability to attract (although the Marxist jargon of recruit would be a better word) blacks to their projects. At other times, the issues of race and concerns for diversity have devolved into screeching accusations leading to self-defeating white guilt. White collectives have even relieved their guilt by seeking out members of the local black community to join them, in fits of tokenism which benefit no one.

Countless hours and much hand-wringing have been devoted to creating effective outreach to black communities. Despite the amount of discussion about anarchists in the United States being mostly white, there has been remarkably little progress in attracting blacks to the anarchy. Some groups have become political Jehovah's Witnesses: white activists going door-to-door in black communities, preaching the benefits of anarchism. This is paternalism at its worst, assuming that it is the "white anarchist's burden" to raise all black people to the lofty heights of our political beliefs. This behavior is especially hypocritical when white anarchists living in impoverished black communities decry other anarchists as racist, while gentrifying entire neighborhoods. Some have suggested toning down anarchist rhetoric and principles, changing the way we dress or the kind of music we listen to, in order not to alienate blacks, as if their community is any less tolerant or more conformist than any other community.

Some have suggested we need to work with authoritarian organizations in black communities in order to persuade them to the anarchist cause. This suggests that authoritarian organizing is typical of black communities. It assumes, implicitly, that only whites can truly appreciate non-hierarchical approaches to organizing and that blacks will be put off by such radical ideas. These attempts, although often sincere, are paternalistic and suggest an underlying disrespect for black communities. They ignore the long history of black anti-authoritarianism, from the slave revolts of Nat Turner to the Black Autonomy movement in the 1980s. Such paternalism also shows a remarkable ignorance of the number of authoritarian white institutions that have taken root in American black communities from evangelical Christianity to the Democratic Party.

It is absurd to believe that black communities, especially those living under the heel of police brutality, are so fragile as to be alienated by outward appearances or tastes in music. For example, after the 2002 riots in Cincinnati, an anarchist contingent planning to take the streets debated whether "blocking up" would confuse black folks and cause more police repression in the local community. These fears proved unfounded. When the masked

anarchists showed up, a local black preacher remarked how he was impressed that the "Seattle kids" (his words) had came to Cincinnati and were marching hand-in-hand with the local community against police brutality. He even asked for a business card(!) to get back in touch with the anarchists for future collaboration. The anarchists also showed several groups of black teenagers how to turn their shirts into masks so that they could avoid police repression and being singled out. This small example illustrates that black communities are potentially eager to make alliances with people with different tactics, clothes, and cultures than their own, if the partnership is one of equals working in solidarity with each other. It should be no surprise that the black communities in Cincinnati reacted positively to white anarchists.

Yet Cincinnati is only one city and many places have never seen similar positive interactions. Some white activists have become so disappointed with the failure of outreach that they reject the attraction of anarchy for liberty-loving folks of any color. They claim that anarchism is simply a Western ideology out of touch with communities of color and thus will never be accepted by them. People who make this claim ignore, at their own risk, the appeal anarchism has for many non-white and non-Western cultures around the world. The fact is that the majority of contemporary anarchists are non-white and non-Western, and anarchism has been colorful for its entire existence. Today, the anarchist communities worldwide are exceptionally diverse: technologically-savvy collectives in South Korea; military resistors in Uganda; and indigenous-groups in Bolivia, Brazil, and Ecuador. Sadly, for most folks in the United States, our images of anarchy have mostly been limited to North America and Europe. North Americans have a lot to learn from these multiple and diverse anarchies across the world, especially how each adapts the basic ideas of anarchism to their pressing local needs. Anarchy is just as relevant to the defense of ancestral land by indigenous tribes or the riots that have swept black communities after acts of police brutality as it is to the more familiar anti-globalization or antigovernment demonstrations.

There are many ways for anarchists to achieve a greater diversity. One way is to create better and more open anarchist projects.

We don't need to change our message, change our clothes, or change our ideals—which aren't in any case limited to a particular class, race, or type of person. We should focus our energy on building successful projects that are open to all people. Some of the resources needed to start these projects will initially come from less oppressed communities, such as white activists or middle class blacks. This doesn't make them wrong, racist, or shortsighted; it simply reflects the historical and cultural reality of State and capitalist oppression. However, anarchists can build counter-structures that can be used by others (including oppressed groups). Relationships of trust between different communities can be built that allow these projects to become more diverse.

Three key elements for successful projects are for them to be open, built on genuine affinity, and effective to the communities involved. By open, we mean that regardless of which group initiates the project, any group can use it if they find the project useful. Openness

THAT'S GETTING KINDA RIDICULOUS ISN'T IT

YEAH, YOU'RE RIGHT.

facilitates the use of these structures by different communities apply-ing their own resistance, in their own voices. The more successful and open a project, the more diverse it will become. People who suffer greater oppression or have fewer expendable resources, such as money and time, will be more willing to take the risk of joining the successful project. Different communities will only commit themselves to projects that are open enough (in resources and possibilities) to allow them to use it in their own ways.

So how exactly does a project become open? There are a num-ber of tested ways in which projects can increase their openness to outside communities. The first is transparency. That means not only how decisions are made but about all aspects of the project: who is involved, why they are involved, and what their goals are. A proj-ect should be as accessible as possible, including ways to connect to people who speak languages other than English: providing bilingual information and propaganda. The last and most difficult for groups is to allow outside communities to use the project without suspicion or micromanaging. This requires mutual trust.

An infoshop can invite black teenagers interested in hip-hop to use the space for open mic slams. If the project is genuinely open, the hip-hoppers' participation will allow the infoshop to grow and evolve in new ways beyond the original intentions of its initiators. The found-ers of a radical infoshop would probably not have been able to develop a hip-hop space, but when the hip-hop "kids" use the space, it expands and cross-pollinates both groups. When the groups trust and respect each other, the infoshop can become a real place for cross-community dialogue and mutual trust to begin.

The hip-hoppers who lack access to a show space may want to use the infoshop on a more regular basis. If the infoshop collective wishes to be open, they should be transparent, letting the kids know what the space is used for, how it started, and what its goals are. This transparency lets the kids make an informed decision about whether the purpose of the infoshop and their own goals are compatible. Again, explicitly anarchist groups should be honest about our politics so that we can avoid misunderstandings down the road. Neither group should have to hide their intentions or politics in order to work together: The infoshop should also have an easy and accessible way for the kids to use the space. Most groups rely on poorly advertised, cliquish meetings to make decisions. Outsiders can be confused and intimidated by these sorts of setups. To be open, infoshops can offer something as simple as a sign-up sheet in the front window Expectations from both groups should be made up front so there is no confusion or misunderstandings later. Being scrutinized by hawklike protectors of a space during an event is never fun and only leads to resentment. The infoshop must trust the kids enough to let them run their own show with as little interference as possible from the collective members. This will allow the hip-hoppers to see the place and their event as their own, and create a sense of value for the project as a whole. A hip-hop event is only one example: different cities have different populations and needs, whether they are day-laborers trying to organize or students planning a walkout.

Openness allows for genuine affinities. Just like people, groups and projects will share natural affinities. For example, the American

Indian Movement organizes their annual anti-Columbus Day protest in Denver with the help of particularly militant Colorado anarchists. These two groups share a history and commitment to direct action. These groups developed their own politics independently yet they share an affinity when it comes to issues and tactics that make them strong allies. Sometimes these alliances happen organically like when the primarily white, young, and anarchist Anti-Racist Action allied with local Somalis in Lewiston, Maine. The arrival of the Nazi thugs brought together this unlikely pairing. For many of the anarchists, it was their first time working in solidarity with Somalis and many people in the Somali community never thought they would have anything in common with anarchists. Affinity, in this case kicking the Nazis out, is a much stronger bond than generic outreach, which chooses alliances solely based on race.

Our projects must also be effective, and this may take more time and effort than openness and affinity. We cannot expect diverse projects overnight. In the mid-Eighties, a pirate radio station was started by techno-geeks and punks on a houseboat in Milwaukee. They started with a mix of punk music and related political and scene reports. Activists from the University of Milwaukee got involved when they found a growing number of students listening to the illegal station. The students used it to promote their campus activism and brought a more overtly political bent to the station. Five years later in 1991, a group of welfare mothers from the Projects organizing against work-fare took to the airwaves to educate people on their issues. Before the FCC shut down the houseboat, the station had the unlikely format of punk rock, campus-based politics, and community organizing. This effective alliance was built slowly over several years. The students and welfare mothers chose to use the station because it was open and shared their affinities, but most importantly because it was an effective tool for getting their voices heard. Many pirate radio stations are started by individuals with time, resources, and some technical skills. Since pirate radio stations are illegal, they often pose some risks. An oppressed community with few expendable resources may think twice before spending their time and labor to risk arrest when they have more pressing needs. An open pirate station, such as the one in Milwaukee, allows folks who have little time and resources to share its benefits. New shows can be developed and if the radio station is successful as a communication medium, it will be used by others to promote their own causes. The increased use of the station will expand and shape its voice, undoubtedly making it more diverse and effective.

There are also other examples that are the reverse of pirate radio. Just as white activists can start a project and non-whites can use it, people of color can start a project that will later attract white anarchists. The Lower East Side and Bronx community gardens are an example of projects initiated by working-class Latinos. The gardens were both successful and open, and they began to attract white activists who helped strengthen and protect them. The two groups also shared an affinity—the desire for green space and community autonomy. Over the last decade, hundreds of gardens were cultivated, occupied, squatted, and defended by militant activists of various backgrounds. Even though the City of New York has bulldozed dozens of gardens to

make way for gentrification, the struggle for the community gardens continues to be a shining example of diversity and openness.

If we are serious about making our communities, cultures, and collectives more racially diverse, then we must be serious about our projects. We must build them with great passion and spend the time needed to nurture them. We must be vigilant to keep them open and capable of evolving as new individuals with similar goals are drawn to them. Taking the hours of unsuccessful outreach back into our hands will enrich our work and strengthen our collectives. This time can also be used to learn about other cultures and find ways we can create healthy relationships. When they are invited, white anarchists can support the initiatives of people of color. Anarchists of every color can transform the debilitating paralysis of white-guilt into a passionate commitment to open projects that folks of any race, ethnicity or background can freely participate and become invested in. Anarchists should abandon the moldy concept of recruitment and focus on creating useful and inspiring projects open to everyone and anyone. Honestly addressing the issue of race will help us build healthier, more diverse communities of resistance.

Courage is Contagious

There is a sacred myth among some anarchists that punks, traveler kids, and their ilk alienate the masses. Some sincerely believe that if we only present a clean-cut face, centuries of anti-anarchist propaganda will evaporate under the light of our wholesome smiles. Patches, tattoos, piercings, masks, black clothing, and even the word "anarchy" itself have been blamed for the perceived apathy most Americans feel about the issues we are fighting for. Some argue that there is too much "individualism" in our communities. These criticisms ignore the strengths the anarchist community actually has.

If we hope to make real impacts in our communities and the outside world we should focus on inspiration, instead of worrying about alienation. The goal of overthrowing the State and ending capitalism is impossible without challenging the traditions and habits of ordinary people's lives; we should not pretend that SUVs or stock options will be a part of our future. Anarchy has always been a gamble with high stakes and impossible odds; and staying active year after year demands cleverness, commitment, and courage. Few of us are brave enough to deal with the overwhelming powers of the dinosaurs alone. Individual courage does not create cultures of resistance. We need to cultivate our collective courage and build heroic communities. We should be the barbarians at the gate, not a horde of inoffensive clones.

Heroic Communities

It is ironic that the greatest boon for anarchy in the public eye of the US during the past few decades has been the tactic of the Black Bloc. The same folks-punks, travelers, greens, and other mangy mis-fits—that the Pollyannas of anarchism would claim are weakening the Movement—have inspired a huge upsurge in anarchist activity in the United States. The Black Blocs of Seattle, Washington, Quebec City (and elsewhere) have inspired people; they were courageous and their solidarity was heroic. Their actions resonated not only with young people but also with many other segments of society from the disempowered black community in Seattle to the unemployed Que-becois youth. While we are constantly told that mainstream Ameri-cans are fearful of the use of violence, the disaffected and excluded understand the urge to destroy property even when it is a tractor driven through a McDonald's!

There have been countless heroic communities from which we can draw inspiration, as we are working to create more of them across the globe today We offer these examples not to glorify the past, but to simply show that *it has been done before and will be done again*. These heroic communities are fairly unique, but they are connected by their practical effects and dedication. These heroic communities each unleashed the imagination of their respective eras and so in-spired unlikely segments of their societies to join them in struggle.

While its currently fashionable to knock traveling kids, these modern day hobos are the sociopolitical descendants of the folks that brought the United States close to full-scale popular revolu-tion—the Industrial Workers of the World. These militants hopped trains from coast to coast, organizing every possible ethnic group and industry into autonomous, interconnected networks of mutual aid. Even though they touted the creation of "One Big Union," a concept that relied on using sheer mass to beat the capitalists, it was their individual and collective acts of solidarity which inspired their contemporaries and still inspire us today. When every (wo)man is an organizer, decentralization and mutual aid are quick to follow. The Industrial Workers of the World didn't wring their hands about violence; they stood their ground against the National Guard,

Pinkertons, the American Legion, mobs, and even the gallows. Now that much of the industrial infrastructure has fled overseas to be replaced by temporary service jobs, perhaps a Post-industrial Ex-Workers of All Worlds is needed.

The grandest of all guerrilla warfare was not carried out in Cuba, China, or even dear old Russia, but in the unlikely country of Champagne and goose liver pâté. Anarchists have overlooked the French Resistance in favor of the heroics of Spain and various Third-World guerillas. The French *Maquis*, along with anti-fascist resistance in nearly every country under the Nazi yoke, was able to inspire thousands of housewives, milkmen, teachers, intellectuals, artists and nearly every segment of society. What is fascinating about the heroic community of the French Maquis is how mundane the lives of the heroes were compared to their secretive exploits. The Allied intelligence officially rejected the Maquis as an "ineffectual, disorganized group of political hooligans" while the collaborators in Vichy were hard pressed to explain to the Reich how military production and law enforcement had been "seriously compromised" by these "fishmongers and ex-students." These communities of resistance, organized in autonomous units in France (and elsewhere) relied on the "medium of inspiration" to spread their message since all propaganda channels

were under Nazi control. They were able to breathe new life in the tired slogan of "Propaganda by the Deed."

For every saboteur in the Maquis, there were dozens of comrades who secured safe housing, food, money and weapons at considerable risk to themselves and their families. These secret supporters spread the idea of resistance in hushed conversations at cafés and over neighborhood fences. All of this was done under the heel of the most efficient repressive police force in history: the Gestapo. The Maquis' heroic acts of sabotage, which they called "Free Acts," stoked the flames of noncompliance among the population, effectively making many ordinary French people a fifth column behind the fascist lines. Every Free Act created an inspirational contagion and even the Gestapo reported, "It is nearly impossible to keep ordinary peasants from talking about these [Free Acts] at bars. It seems to create an atmosphere of resistance in unexpected quarters."

Today we have short-lived coalitions like the "Turtles & Teamsters of Seattle," but nothing compares to the unlikely alliance between runaway slaves, swamp-dwelling natives, and Mexican peasants known as the Seminole Nation. It is wrong to consider the Seminole Nation a coalition in the modern sense. Instead, it created a cultural fusion that took linguistic, sociological, and political aspects from all three groups to create an unique community of resistance whose existence stretched from before the creation of the United States until well after the Civil War: The Seminoles inspired fear among British soldiers, the US federal government, slavers, Texas rangers, hierarchical Native American tribes, and the Mexican military. They were not only successful in frustrating their enemies, but provided a wellspring of hope for those fleeing authoritarian tribes and the horror of slavery. How was this possible in a time before mass media? The answer is simple: the heroic acts of the Seminoles and their unswerving militant resistance made them legends in their own lifetimes. Their reputation motivated oppressed peoples to engage in equally heroic acts such as running away from their slavemasters and traveling hundreds of miles as fugitives to join this new community. What is so fascinating about this unique tribe is that they carried on their resistance far longer than many other tribes in the Americas and arguably with greater success than even the Plains Indians. They dreamed of a land of their own and fought to secure it against many foes.

These are just a few examples of heroic communities overlooked by anarchists, but there are many more. There are examples to be drawn from French mutineers of the first World War, pirates of both the Caribbean and North Africa, slave revolts in the New World, the English Diggers, the fiery sailors of frozen Kronstadt, and many more whose stories have been stripped from history books. Despite their geographical and historical differences, they share a host of common characteristics though no group probably contained all of these characteristics. First, they place an emphasis on the overall community as opposed to the personality of spokesperson. Second, the community is open to outsiders, new ideas, and innovative tactics. Third, the community develops its own mongrel and unique culture of decentralized resistance. Finally, these communities make radical change the heart of their tactics, message, and culture.

From the Maquis to Seminoles, it is hard to find leaders in these cultures of resistance. Governments do not understand leaderless resistance, and they often ridiculously create false leaders and masterminds. Famously, the US and the Mexican governments tried to portray Wild Cat, a brilliant warrior and strategist, as the leader of the Seminoles. He rejected any such status and said, "I speak for myself, for I am free. Each of the others also speak for themselves. We are a choir of free voices that will drown out your lies." Similarly the French Maquis refused to send leaders to negotiate with either the Vichy government or the Allies. Frustrated, both governments anointed DeGalle as the "leader" despite the fact that he actually fled France to England. Leaderless resistance was both a tactical and political necessity for these heroic communities and remains for the ones we create today.

Heroic communities tend not to erect inflexible boundaries between themselves and the rest of the world; instead they are open to outsiders and outside ideas. They are marked by their flexible nature when compared to the societies that they are in opposition against. Out of this flux of people from various backgrounds with differing ideas of what they want from life, heroic communities create sustaining and nurturing cultures. These mongrel groups possessed an egalitarian openness that created space for new ideas and tactics to develop rapidly. They sought to create a new and free society and were willing to fight effectively for it. They rejected tactical centralization, refusing to line up their forces on a field against numerically superior and better-equipped government forces. Instead, they utilized the flexibility and innovation of autonomous affinity groups (cells, crews, and bands) working in concert. These communities refused to water down their ideals or tone down their tactics in order to gain popular support. Their message was meant to intimidate their enemies, not to bolster recruitment. They attracted folks precisely because they were genuine; they were offering real and meaningful change.

We can already hear the shouts of the critics, "But they all failed!" And, sadly, these critics are partially right. None of these communities of resistance continue today in a recognizable form: the Seminoles are best known for their casinos and the Wobblies today are a shadow of their precursors. Yet during their heyday these heroic communities created the sorts of relationships and fierce resistance that most of us aspire to today. Instead of placing them in the dustbin of history as interesting failures or worshiping them, we can learn from their methods and mistakes. Courage is contagious. Our challenge is to be confident enough to form heroic communities here and now because freedom is as universal as the world we all inhabit and as different as each of its inhabitants.

Propaganda by the Need, Propaganda by the Deed!

Even the Angels and Dogs Have Masks: A Folktale

(As told to CrimethInc. Mercenary Regina de Bray)

> *"And then the tiny mouse saw the tiny bit of cheese,*
> *the milk, and the tiny fish, everything that he want-*
> *ed was in the tiny kitchen, and he could not get there*
> *because the tiny cat would not allow it. And then the*
> *tiny mouse said "Enough!" and he grabbed a machine*
> *gun and shot the tiny cat."*
> *—The Story of the Tiny Mouse and the Tiny Cat,*
> *a Zapatista children's story*

Be Realistic...

At its heart, anarchy is helping your friends for no greater end than your friendship—we anarchists call this mutual aid. Although it sounds easy, all the powers that be discourage us from helping our friends. As the capitalists would have it, the world is a cold and desolate place, where everyone greets each other as potential competitors and enemies, because there is *simply not enough to go around.* Not enough of everything—not enough money, not enough time, not enough food, not enough love—and soon enough, not even enough clean air or clean water. In such a world, who can afford friends? The only way to banish this dysfunctional thinking is to go out into the world and disprove it with your own life. That's exactly what we set out to do.

Demand the Impossible!

Sometimes, we don't ever meet our friends. We just hear about them, read about them, listen to their music, and no matter how distant they seem we feel a bond that miraculously crosses space and time. One day a neighbor told me that the Zapatistas, an armed indigenous rebellion that stormed into the front-page of global news on the day of the ratification in 1994 of the North American Free Trade Agreement (NAFTA), would appreciate some computers and other general help.

I looked her in straight in the eye and said,"I'll be down there as soon as possible." And I meant it. The Zapatistas' revolt has inspired the entire world, and while we had never personally met them, nor been to Chiapas, if they needed something and it was within our ability to get, we would certainly try. As most Americans realize, Western society is so wasteful that you can daily find perfectly good things thrown away. Many of our friends have taken advantage this extravagance by dumpster-diving. Usually dumpster-diving is limited to merely food found in dumpsters, barely enough to feed our hungry bellies and some left over for Food Not Bombs. However: the rich throw computers into the trash like stale bread as soon as the newest model comes out, despite the fact that millions would love to use them. So, we decided to dumpster-dive some computers and somehow make our way to Chiapas. *Nothing could be easier.*

There were several problems, the first being a severe lack of computers. Never ones to let something as dreary as reality curb our enthusiasm, we began to pray to the ever-shifty patron spirits of thieves and hobos to deliver unto us working computers. Soon after we completed our dark rituals, several computers incarnated themselves to answer our prayers. It turned out that a group of activists was willing to donate some old computers they had been given by a non-profit group. Unfortunately, we were in Boston, recovering from yet another anarchist street protest, and the computers were on the West Coast! Without fear, a merry band of companions rose to the occasion to bring needed supplies and goodwill to Mexico.

With little in the way of possessions and—as usual—no money, we hopped trains across the Arctic North, making our way to the West Coast solely on a large pack of oats, which we promptly gave away to an indigenous family we met along the way who were hitchhiking to Seattle. We picked up the computers from the friendly, hip West Coast activists and realized to our dismay that without an automobile, we had no way to transport them down the street, much less to Chiapas. Again, our lack of planning seemed to doom us! We couldn't hitchhike or trainhop with them, and our trusty van was stranded in Boston.

Luckily a small horde of primitivists was passing through en route to Arizona, on a tour to promote the destruction of civilization. Although we reasoned computers were surely included under the category of civilization, once we explained our scheme, they offered to lend a hand. Despite the irony of their situation the band of anarcho-primitivists were more than willing to help us, and in turn the Zapatistas, by strapping the computers to the top of their van, taking them one step closer to their final destination.

In search of our long-lost van, we got a ride across California and Arizona, funded purely by an orgy of gas-thievery and scams, until other members of our ragged crew managed to get the van (loaded with even more computers picked up on the way from a shady inside job at a well-known Washington, D.C. corporation) to our secret base in the suburbs of Atlanta and ready it for the trip. The van, brimming with anarchists, began its slow journey, breaking an axle and having nearly flipped due to the weight of the computers. One of the computers was bartered along the way to a car mechanic for a used axle in Mississippi, and we continued our odyssey.

We made it to Arizona, picked up the computers from the green anarchists, and hit another snag. The border itself seemed insurmountable. After all, you're not supposed to truck a vanload of computers into a foreign country and not expect to have questions asked by the border guards! Luckily, we were aided by a group of Quakers in collaboration with a union of Mexican anarcho-syndicalist sweatshop workers who maneuvered the goods across the border without a problem. After giving several of the computers to the union, we drove to Chiapas triumphant. The truly remarkable feat was that we did this with few resources besides our maniacal unemployment and the legend of the Zapatistas. It only happened because of the help of young balaclava-clad anarcho-primitivists, a disgruntled D.C. middle manager, a Mississippi mechanic, Mexican sweatshop workers, and elderly pacifists: a network of friends capable of doing the impossible for an armed indigenous rebellion. Through mutual aid, we helped create a network of friends that crossed an entire continent. The only question is: What's next?

After the journey I was sitting with notepad in hand writing down the license plates of the police cars and military trucks as they drove by the Zapatista village. Above me was what was at one time a church, and was now something completely different. For while the church was full of pictures of angels, these brown-skinned angels had bandanas hiding their faces. And where there would have normally been a picture of Christ, or at least the Virgin Mary, there was the Virgin of Guadalupe with a mask cradling a gun like a child. I asked Manuel, a stocky Zapatista local whose job was to let only friends through the gate and who had the goodwill to put up with my broken Spanish, why the angels had masks. He said "Even the angels have masks—they're Zapatista angels."

Like all the autonomous communities I visited, there was a pack of mangy dogs living on the edge of town running about, self-evidently up to no good. "Ahh…" I began jokingly "whose dogs are those?" Manuel responded, "Those are perros autonomos, even the dogs are Zapatistas." I asked him why they weren't wearing masks. "We all have masks. The angels, the dogs, the corn, the Virgin Mary, the children, the elders—we all have masks. Sometimes we are not wearing them, but the masks are always there."

Infrastructure for the Hell of It!

Over the last decade there has been a lot of passionate discussion amongst anarchists about the need for infrastructure in North America. Despite this profound desire for an explicitly anarchist infrastructure, there has been little collective activity or even clear visions about what this could look like.

Infrastructure seems just too damn big to think about, much less accomplish. When we think about infrastructure, things like transportation, communication networks, power, sewage, and housing come to mind. Or else we imagine giant public works projects that cost millions of dollars, require the labor of thousands of people, and often take decades or more to realize. No wonder most of us are paralyzed by the idea of infrastructure! Worse, this paralysis leads to a great deal of skepticism about the possibility of an anarchist society's chance of thriving. However; there is a different kind of infrastructure and it is small, free, and festive—an infrastructure very alien to the massive dinosaur infrastructure around us today. What we are working for is a *counter-structure* that will allow us to live not only outside of, but against, the current infrastructure.

Counter-structure happens, without even planning for it. It is insidious and creeps into our projects on kitten paws. Counter-structure organically grows in reaction to the immediate physical environment and current events, which is why Food Not Bombs (FNB) is so popular in America but not in a country like Scotland where there are many soup kitchens and government aid programs. FNB, in particular, has a folk anarchist quality because it is *more* than just infrastructure to fulfill immediate needs; it empowers all who take part in its genuine relationships based on mutual aid.

The homeless (or home-free, depending on her perspective) woman who comes to Food Not Bombs for the free food has the opportunity to begin cooking the food with the group and empowering herself. After a short amount of time, she can become integral to the whole endeavor and other projects as well. This process is the exact opposite of the government (or church) sponsored soup-kitchens that immobilize hungry people, turning them into passive consumers taking handouts from staff who function as specialized producers. Food Not

WE DON'T WANT A PIECE OF YOUR FUCKIN CAKE!

Bombs is only one of a number of counter-structural developments in our culture already: infoshops, free spaces, Indymedia, Internet services, health and medic collectives, and food cooperatives. Although the current anarchist infrastructure is far from perfect (we are definitely in the need of a few good anarchist surgeons!) it does exist outside of textbooks and wishful thinking. Unlike oppressive dinosaur infrastructure, anarchist counter-structure's real strength lies in its ability to inspire others to replicate and expand itself.

There is no master cabal organizing the three-hundred plus Food Not Bombs or mad genius organizing the dozens of Indymedias across the globe. We can all be the Johnny and Jane Appleseeds of anarchist counter-structure. We do this by harvesting good ideas and strategies from across the globe and replicating them on the local level. And while our passions and ideas should be brash, we should also be inspired by our day-to-day victories. People need to feel encouraged to start small, realizing that infrastructure begets infrastructure.

If your neighborhood has hungry people, do not fret over getting a non-profit license from the State, looking for a place to rent, or deciding how a food pantry will be run. Start small. Get some friends together, look for food you do not need or can easily replace, and make a meal. Throw a party with free food for anyone that wants it by taking a bag of sandwiches to the park or the subway and passing them out. Maybe everyone around you is sick of the corporate news. Go onto Indymedia or infoshop.org and grab a news posting or item, print copies, and give them away during your lunch break to discuss it. If there is no place for a meeting, open your home, squat a table at the library, or meet in a park.

Decentralized infrastructure can be every bit as effective (and perhaps more) than behemoth centralized infrastructures. There are numerous examples of decentralized infrastructures that have had huge impacts on hundreds of thousands of lives. Balinese irrigation is decentralized but it provides water to thousands of farms and is a key component in the island's ability to feed itself. In Bolivia, simple community wells created by a handful of unskilled laborers in each neighborhood provide as much as 5% of the potable water needs for the entire country. They accomplish this with more regular service than the State-owned water company. And it's free! Community gardens and small scale Community Supported Agriculture (CSAs) are finding new ways for inner cities and small farmers and gardeners to connect outside of the exploitive agribusiness industry. Dollar vans and gypsy cabs, which provide quick, cheap rides for regular folks, are routinely more effective in providing transportation needs

for under-served communities like Brooklyn and the Bronx than huge, bloated, public municipal transportation systems.

The beauty of small-scale infrastructure is that it is participatory. Not only does it provide a needed service (food, space, water, transportation, and so on) but it is directly responsible to the community it serves and also allows people to learn skills from each other It draws on the needs of the community and the already present local resources and skills. This is the underlying advantage of decentralized infrastructure: it brings together mutual aid and the do-it-yourself ethic in a way that empowers both the participants and the benefactors, blurring the line between producer and consumer. Instead of being a mere service, decentralized infrastructure actually empowers those it serves while being able to immediately respond to the changing needs of the community.

Why should anarchists spend their limited resources and energy working on infrastructure when there are other projects that need to be done? Why create counter-structures while there are protests to organize, art installations to be readied, bands to see, and manifestos to be written? What is the political value in cruising the streets in a beat up van taking old ladies to the local CSA for a sack of turnips? Why open up a free babysitting service as the nation gears up for another insane war? What could be the possible political motive for opening and fixing up a squat for a few families when over 35,000 folks are sleeping on our city's streets? Who cares about a crudely Xeroxed zine when most Americans get their news from television moguls? Aren't there better things we anarchists should be doing?

In short, the answer is a resounding "No." These more "important things" are impossible without a viable anarchist infrastructure. You can't stop a war, shut down an IMF meeting, or create a free and egalitarian society without an effective decentralized infrastructure. The good news is that this infrastructure allows you to be more effective in your struggles against the war, the State, and the entire capitalist system. To get people onto the streets, we have to ensure there is also shelter, food, legal, communications, and medics on those streets. We are not only political beings but flesh and blood animals that need food, water, a place to rest our heads, and health to engage in social and political work.

Infrastructure is not only something that large bureaucracies can provide. For most of recorded history humans have provided for the needs of their communities without hierarchical and coercive institutions. Society is complex but this is mostly a result of the tendency of the authorities hoarding power and wealth. The more explicitly anarchist infrastructure we have, the more time, energy and resources there are to wage a serious resistance. For these reasons building this infrastructure is meaningful political and cultural work. There are many untapped skills, materials, and ideas in our communities if we are only willing to search them out.

To Sir, With a Grenade

"Mutiny is the Conscience of War"
—common graffiti by soldiers in the trenches of WWI

Our future isn't over and for many of us, the present hasn't even begun. If we accept only the official histories of high school textbooks we have no reason to treat the past as anything but yet another dead hand that weighs us down. But history can be a living cultural memory that can be re-remembered and re-experienced. We can challenge it on new fronts and, when it is no longer needed, abandon it.

What kind of histories can anarchists look for? Well, they hide in the strangest of places. History is nothing more than the sum of the collective experiences of the world, and we are just as much part of it as anything in a history book. If we can uncover the voices bulldozed by official histories, reading behind and between the lines of the official texts, we can discover together a history worth remembering. Our local research squad has uncovered a history of resistance found in the most authoritarian and unexpected of all environments: the military.

> *Mutiny: (V.) Rebellion against lawful authority.*
> *—Webster's dictionary*

The history of mutiny is a history of conscious rebellion against military hierarchy. The study of mutiny is far more instructive than the study of the tired, imperial victories of states and their murderous armies. Since the first documented mutiny against Julius Caesar by Gallic conscripts over two thousand years ago, mutineers have played an important role in checking the absolutist and militaristic dreams of would-be emperors. Mutinies have occurred in every major war on every continent. There is an undeniable thread connecting mutineers throughout history to our modern day struggles—a rejection of totalitarian authority and a fierce demand for freedom.

Mutinies aren't merely random acts of disgruntled soldiers, mutinies are political uprisings. These range from the rejection of British cultural imperialism by Muslims in the Sepoy Mutiny, black soldiers fighting against their racist superiors on the USS Chicago, unpaid immigrants rising up against the Union during US Civil War, anarchist sailors rejecting communist tyranny during the famous Kronstadt Uprising, to the burning of barracks by maltreated soldiers in the Papua Mutinies of 1999 and 2002.

Free For All

> *"Discipline is the soul of an army."*
> —George Washington

Most writings on mutinies come from official military reports and tribunal transcripts. Despite these biased reports, the authorities cannot deny or erase why mutinies have for so long kept generals from getting a restful sleep. The Vietnam "conflict" was marked by full-scale mutinies against the US military. When an American soldier in Vietnam killed a superior officer, the term "fragging" came into use. Although the term simply meant that a fragmentation grenade was used in the murder, it later became an all-encompassing term for such actions. Hundreds or thousands of "fraggings" occurred during Vietnam, but the precise number is uncertain. Dr. Terry Anderson of Texas A&M University wrote: "The US Army itself does not know exactly how many [...] officers were murdered. But they know at least 600 were murdered, and then they have another 1400 that died mysteriously. Consequently, by early 1970, the army was at war not with the enemy but with itself." Many pacifists would argue in favor of staying out of the military but activists with the courage to spread their ideas in the ranks and the courage to put a bullet in an officer's head could potentially be as effective as yet another peace demonstration in Washington, D.C. Diversity of tactics, indeed.

Vietnam mutineers were more sophisticated than their ancestors, in both their use of media and non-hierarchical structures to ferment mutiny. At best count, there were at least 144 underground newspapers published on or aimed at US military bases in this country and overseas. These journals were not mere gripe-sheets that poked fun in the "Beetle Bailey" tradition against the brass but intelligent and passionate calls for resistance. "In Vietnam," writes the Ft. Lewis-McChord Free Press, "the Lifers, the Brass, are the true Enemy, not the Viet-Cong." Another West Coast sheet advises readers: "Don't desert. Go to Vietnam and kill your commanding officer." They even developed proto-infoshops right on military bases in the US and abroad. By 1971, there were at least 11 (some military researchers suggest as many as 26) on-base antiwar "coffee houses" which supplied GIs with rock music, cheap coffee, antiwar literature, how-to tips on desertion, and similar disruptive counsels while serving to organize deeper resistances inside the armed forces.

All of this agitation and organization led not only to newspapers, infoshops, and the frequent fragging of officers, but also to the serious crippling of the US's ability to wage war in Vietnam. In 1970, the Army had 65,643 deserters, or roughly the equivalent of four infantry divisions, and a yearly increase of 12% in the Desertion/Refusal Rate (DRR). Despite having some of the most repressive laws, liberal use of executions, and a 230% increase in the number of Military Police Officers, the US Army was initially helpless to stop the spreading mutiny in its ranks. In addition to mass desertions and specific fraggings, soldiers used sabotage to disrupt the military. One famous case involved sailors who damaged an aircraft carrier so badly by pouring saltwater into the computers, removing nuts from bolts, and even flooding the ballast holds, that it had to be scuttled before leaving San Francisco.

To stop a full-scale insurrection, the Department of Defense Intelligence and Propaganda divisions stepped in during the summer of 1971 with their new "cultural front." They made officers grow sideburns, started teaching classes on current pop music, produced slick glossy "counterculture" zines, and opened up Patriot Clubs that not only served cheap coffee and alcohol but also specialized in heroin. The army in Vietnam, once a fertile bed of resistance against military authority, was re-domesticated through numbing drugs and so-called alternative culture. The mutineers lost their momentum and the war ended with a drop in DRR rates, fewer fraggings, and less military sabotage. The military had learned its lesson. Today the US relies on an all volunteer army, superior technology, and foreign allies that are easily coerced and don't have to come home in body bags to American mothers. The military learned culture was a stronger tool than firing squads. Just as the army learns from its mistakes, so must anarchists who would dismantle the military once and for all.

RAND Corp., one of the more intelligent neurons of the modern dinosaur brain, suggests that the inherent strength of the modern day mutiny undoubtedly lies in the strength of a decentralized model. Mutineers, leaderless and without any tangible gains other than venting a deep resentment, are especially immune to traditional control structures. The report, based on recent mutinies in the Georgia Republic and mutinies in Russia's failed invasion of Afghanistan, goes on to say that mutineers are immune to traditional patriotic propaganda and calls for civil service. The report suggests that mutineers may also "infect" civilian populations with "fake bravery" and the "underdog principle" leading to "substantial challenges to other [non-military] forms of authority." RAND goes on to suggest initiatives like the 1971 DoD "Cultural Front" may need to be extended to "recruiting bases in [civilian communities] [...] where proper discipline can be managed before the recruit ever signs the papers in the neighborhood recruiting office."

What the RAND report misses is that mutineers are really no different than civilian populations. They are mostly conscripts, people of color, and the poor. These are the people deemed most expendable by the power elite. All mutinies have been about survival and justice and this resonates with all of those who have felt the brunt of oppression regardless of their particular role in the military machine.

Mutiny is not revolution. It is an act, or a series of acts, that takes direct action against oppression in order to *get rid of the captain*. For non-soldiers, any form of lawful authority could be considered "the captain" whether it is a cop, a foul teacher, or your domineering boss. Unlike the image of the glorious Revolution, mutinies take place in the immediate environment on a small scale without too much regard for what happens after the mutiny. In places where oppression is overwhelming, such as the battlefield, mutineers are often opportunistic or spontaneous, without any specific political motivation other than the most important one: survival. These revolts are anarchistic by nature—they reject authority in the most visceral and concrete way. Mutinies are micro-environments where people reject the rules, reject appointed leaders, and anyone else who has taken control.

One vital difference between ordinary folks and the mutineers is that mutineers are a highly armed force serving as the linchpin of State power. If it can take place in one of the most important sanctuaries of the State then it can take place anywhere. If we take

2015 STOCK MARKET RIOT

diversity of tactics seriously, the next time the State starts, besides holding a peace sign or a teach-in, we might contemplate joining the army!

Mutiny as Revolt Against Authority in Everyday Life

Today few in the US today are literally forced to serve in the military. Instead of conscripts, the State has a mercenary force made up of the poorest and most oppressed peoples of our country: people of color and the poor. These are folks who under other circumstances would be our sisters and brothers in arms against the State. Over a billion dollars each year is spent by the US Armed Forces on slick commercials, school recruiting, and other forms of sophisticated manipulation to con the poorest and least educated of our population into sacrificing their freedoms and lives to enforce the imperial order.

Since before World War II, the State has been sophisticated in using culture against us to control our lives. There is an inherent risk, as RAND and others have pointed out, in using large armed forces to keep control of the populace: namely, giving weapons to possible mutineers and insurrectionists. Today for those outside of the military, the bayonet of WWI for keeping soldiers in line has been replaced by the boss and union leader for keeping working people subdued. Still, mutiny lives in folks' resistance to compulsory work in the United States, even if such resistance is scattered or is boiling just

HAIL TO THE CHIEF?

beneath the surface. Yet the days of worker militancy are not necessarily stuck in the past. Instead of relying on modern lap-dog unions, working folks have recently been fighting back. The workplace has been the crucible of a number of everyday mutinies from wildcat strikes to expropriation of materials, sabotage, and even mass desertion (such as walkouts). When these acts are done in solidarity with other struggles, such as the longshoremen shutting down the docks of the entire West Coast during the anti-WTO protests, mutiny is a powerful weapon against capitalists and the State.

Where else can mutiny take place? Our schools have a barely hidden agenda of indoctrination for the creation of good workers and more passive consumers. The military demotion has been replaced with the high school permanent record. Against the grain, students have been in various states of mutiny since at least the 1960s when Berkeley high-school students overthrew their teachers and turned three schools into autonomous zones. In 2002, more than 20,000 students from New York City, mostly Black and Latino teens from the boroughs, deserted their high schools and middle schools to take their grievances to the street. During the Second Gulf War, students all across Britain went on strike, militantly blocking roads and otherwise putting their elders to shame with their commitment to direct action and genuine autonomy. Today, thousands of underground newspapers and zines fill the halls and minds of the rebellious. It is only a matter of time before the next wave of mutiny challenges school systems across the world.

The brig has been replaced by the criminal in-justice system. The dream deferred that is America can be barely contained by these various prisons, both of the social and literal kind. Attica is just the most well-known of prison uprisings; there have been hundreds in recent memory. Everywhere in the gulags of America, prisoners are arming themselves with books, discussion circles, and passion to live free within a totalitarian environment. Prisoners have become more militant in the past years, organizing themselves into study circles and other mutual aid groups. In the miserable environment of prisons, there are still signs of resistance, as shown by the efforts of prisoners to create unions and to educate themselves.

Make no mistake, lawful authority—even in its civilian disguises—is as repressive and dangerous as military authoritarianism. The mutiny has never ended. We should be willing to stand up to any authority that is willing to throw away our lives and passions in the name of imperialism, consumerism, or patriotism. When the never-ending Orwellian War on Terror has militarized everyday life in the cities and suburbs, we can all be mutineers. People are already deserting their workplaces, schools, and malls in ever growing numbers. When desertion is not an option, sabotage is a must.

We can refuse the orders of political leaders and Wall Street corporate shills. Instead, let's focus our energy on creating new forms of communication, publishing even more passionate propaganda, and building more infrastructures and autonomous spaces. Whether we are working stiffs, students, the unemployed, or prisoners, we are experts on our own oppression. It is in our power to desert the stores that sell our lives cheap, sabotage the workplaces that enslave not only our bodies but also our minds, and frag the deadening dogma of our school systems. Take aim not only at NCOs but CEOs, MBAs, FCCs, ADAs, and anyone else wishing to regiment your life! We must be brave enough to mutiny against the elites' lock-step cultural front whether it comes in the form of MTV, Starbucks, or "alternative fashion." In the past mutineers were armed with their grenades, their bayonets and their M-16s; today we are armed with our desires, our intelligence, a pocket full of stones, and maybe more.

SOMEONE IS ALWAYS FASTER...
THAT'S CAPITALISM, YOU KNOW?

RECIPE'S FOR AFFINITY GROUPS©

FROM ANARCHIST'S COOKBOOK
An EXCELLENT SOURCE FOR RADICALS
STEAL ME

AFFINITY GROUPS ARE EXCELLENT FORM FOR ALL OCCASIONS: LOCAL PROJECT, INTERNATIONAL CAMPAIGN SOCIAL GATHERINGS, DIRECT ACTIONS, ETC. THEY COME IN MANY VARIETIES AND SIZES, FROM ON-THE-STREET-DIRECT ACTION (POPULAR IN SEATTLE, PRAGUE AND QUEBEC CITY) TO MANAGING AN INFOSHOP, REGARDLESS OF THE FINAL DISH, THESE AFFINITY GROUPS HAVE GENERAL TRAITS IN COMMON WHICH HAVE MADE THEM SO POPULAR WITH THE CIRCLE A GROUP. HERE ARE A FEW THINGS THAT YOU SHOULDN'T FORGET WHEN PUTTING TOGETHER YOUR OWN AFFINITY GROUP...

TAKE 3-10 (MORE OR LESS) INDIVIDUALS...

SOUR

CRUSTY

"I THINK I'M LOSING SELF-- RESPECT -- HAND OVER THE BOTTLE!"

? - 1 MAIN PROJECT (add more as necessary)

"...1 DASH OF FUN

3 CUPS OF RESPECT (like bottles when you're HARD) (1 FUCK, IT DOESN'T MATTER)

"I THINK I RE- SPECT MYSELF A LITTLE BIT MORE NOW..."

"SIMMER UNTIL CONSENSUS IS REACHED

ASSHOLE MORON

Dita

LA LA LA

A WEEKLY CHANCE TO SOCIALIZE (minimum)

The End of Arrogance:
Decentralization in Anarchist
Organizing

For too long, anarchist projects have been mismanaged by arrogant fantasies of mass. We have unconsciously adopted the dinosaur (statist, capitalist, and authoritarian) belief that "bigger equals better" and that we must tailor our actions and groups towards this end. Despite our intuitive understandings that large organizations rarely accomplish more than small, tight groups working together, the desire for mass remains strong. Let's re-examine how we organize projects in order to awake from the nightmare of bureaucracy, centralization, and ineffective projects. The rejection of mass organizations as the be-all, end-all of organizing is vital for the creation and rediscovery of possibilities for empowerment and effective anarchist work.

The Tyranny of Structure

Most mass structures are a result of habit, inertia, and the lack of creative critique. Desire for mass is accepted as common sense in the same way it is "common sense" that groups must have leaders, or that they must make decisions by voting. Even anarchists have been tricked into accepting the necessity of superstructures and large organizations for the sake of efficiency, mass, and unity. These superstructures have become a badge of legitimacy and they are often the only conduits by which outsiders—whether the media, the police, or the traditional Left—can understand us. The result is an alphabet soup of mega-groups that largely exist to propagate themselves and sadly do little else. Unfortunately, we haven't just been tricked into accepting superstructures as the overriding venue of our work: many of us have gone along willingly because the promise of mass is a seductive one.

Large coalitions and superstructures have become the *modus operandi* not only for Leftist groups in general but also for anarchist enterprises. They appeal to activists' arrogant fantasies of mass. Even our best intentions and wildest dreams are often crowded out by visions of the black clad mob storming the Bastille or the IMF headquarters.

The price of the arrogant dream of mass is appallingly high and the promised returns never come. Superstructures such as federations, centralized networks, and mass organizations demand energy and resources to survive. They are not perpetual-motion machines that produce more energy than is poured into them. In a community of limited resources and energy like ours, a superstructure can consume most of these available resources, rendering the entire group ineffective. Mainstream non-profits have recently illustrated this tendency. Large organizations like the Salvation Army commonly spend 2/3 of their monies (and even larger amounts of their labor) on simply maintaining their existence: officers, outreach, meetings, and public appearance. At best, only 1/3 of their output actually goes to their stated goals. The same trend is replicated in our political organizations.

We all know that most large coalitions and superstructures have exceedingly long meetings. Here's a valuable exercise: the next time you find yourself bored by an overlong meeting, count the number of people in attendance. Then multiply that number by how long the meeting lasts—this will give you the number of people-hours devoted to keeping the organization alive. Factor in travel time, outreach time and the propaganda involved in promoting the meeting and that will give you a rough estimate of the amount of hours consumed by the greedy maw of the superstructure. After that nightmarish vision, stop and visualize how much could be accomplished if this immense amount of time, resources and energy were actually spent on the project at hand instead of what is so innocently referred to as "activism."

Affinity or Bust

Not only are superstructures wasteful, but they also require that we mortgage our ideals and affinities. By definition, coalitions seek to create and enforce agendas. These are not merely agendas for a particular meeting but larger priorities for what type of work is important. Within non-anarchist groups, this prioritization often leads to an organizational hierarchy to ensure that all members of the group promote the overall agenda.

A common example is the role of the media person or spokesman (and it is almost always a man) whose comments are accepted as the opinion for dozens, hundreds, or sometimes thousands of people. In groups without a party line or platform, we certainly shouldn't accept any other person speaking for us—as individuals, affinity groups, or collectives. While the delusions of media stars and spokes people are merely annoying, superstructures can lead to scenarios with much graver consequences. In mass mobilizations or actions, the tactics of an entire coalition are often decided by a handful of people. Many of the disasters of particular recent mobilizations can be squarely blamed on the centralization of information and tactical decisions on a tiny cadre of individuals within the larger coalition (which might include dozens of collectives and affinity groups). For anarchists, such a concentration of influence and power in the hands of a few is simply unacceptable, yet all too often we go along with it for the sake of building alliances.

It has long been a guiding principle of anarchist philosophy that people should engage in activities based on their affinities and that our work should be meaningful, productive, and enjoyable. This is the hidden benefit of voluntary association. It is arrogant to believe that members in a large structure, which again can number in the hundreds or thousands of people, should all have identical affinities and ideals. It is arrogant to believe that through discussion and debate, any one group should convince the others that their particular agenda will be meaningful, productive, and enjoyable for all.

Liberty Trust, and True Solidarity

> *"All liberty is based on Mutual Trust."*
> *—Sam Adams*

If we seek a truly liberated society in which to flourish, we must also create a trusting society. Cops, armies, laws, governments, religious specialists, and all other hierarchies are essentially based on

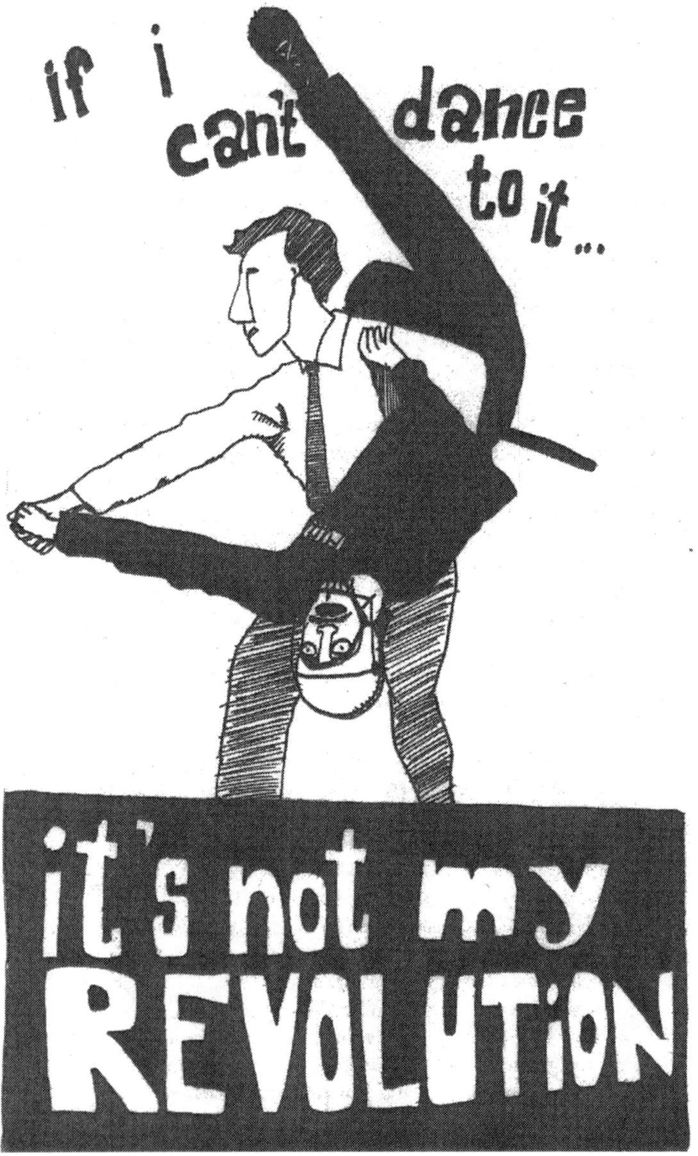
if i can't dance to it...
it's not my REVOLUTION

mistrust. Superstructures and coalitions mimic this basic distrust that is so rampant and detrimental in the wider society. In the grand tradition of the Left, large organizations today feel that due to their size or mission, they have a right to micromanage the decisions and actions of all its members. For many activists, this feeling of being something larger than themselves fosters an allegiance to the organization above all. These are the same principles that foster nationalism and patriotism. Instead of working through and building initiatives and groups that we ourselves have created and are based in our own communities, we work for a larger organization with diluted goals, hoping to convince others to join us. This is the trap of the Party, the three letter acronym group, and the large coalition.

In large groups, power is often centralized, controlled by officers (or certain working groups) and divvied out, as it would be done by any bureaucratic organization. In fact, a great deal of its energies are devoted to guarding this power from others in the coalition. In groups that attempt to attract anarchists (such as anti-globalization and anti-war coalitions) this centralization of power is transferred to certain high profile working groups such as Media or Tactical, even though the Housing, Food, Medical, and Legal groups usually do a better job. Regardless of how it appears on the outside, superstructures foster a climate in which tiny minorities have disproportionate influence over others in the organization.

As anarchists, we ordinarily reject all notions of centralized power and power hoarding. We should be critical of anything that demands the realignment of our affinities and passions for the good of an organization or abstract principle like the overused term "unity" We should guard our autonomy with the same ferocity with which the superstructures wish to strip us of it.

Mutual aid has long been the guiding principle by which anarchists work together. The paradox of mutual aid is that we can only protect our own autonomy by trusting others to be autonomous. Superstructures do the opposite and seek to limit autonomy and work based on affinity in exchange for playing on our arrogant fantasies and the doling out of power. Decentralization is the basis of not only autonomy (which is the hallmark of liberty), but also of trust. To have genuine freedom, we have to allow others to engage in their work based on their desires and skills while we do the same. We can hold no power from them or try to coerce them into accepting our agenda. The successes that we have in the streets and in our local communities almost always come from groups working together: not because they are coerced and feel duty-bound, but out of genuine mutual aid and solidarity.

We should continue to encourage others to do their work in coordination with ours. In anarchist communities, we should come together as equals: deciding for ourselves with whom we wish to form affinity groups or collectives. In accordance with that principle, each affinity group should be able to freely choose which groups they want to work. These alliances might last for weeks or for years, for a single action or for a sustained campaign, with two groups, or two hundred. Our downfall is when the larger organization becomes our focus, not the work that it was created for. We should work together, but only with equal status and with no outside force, neither the State, god, nor some coalition, determining the direction or shape of the work we do. Mutual trust allows us to be generous with mutual aid. Trust promotes relationships where bureaucracies, formal procedures, and large meetings promote alienation and atomization. We can afford to be generous with our limited energies and resources while working with others because these relationships are voluntary and based on a principle of equality. No group should sacrifice their affinity, autonomy, or passions for the privilege to work with others. Just as we are very careful with whom we would work in an affinity group, we should not offer to join a coalition with groups with whom we do not share mutual trust.

We can and should work with other groups and collectives, but only on the basis of autonomy and trust. It is unwise and undesirable to demand that particular group must agree with the decisions of every other group. During demonstrations, this principle is the foundation of the philosophy of "diversity of tactics." It is bizarre that anarchists demand diversity of tactics in the streets but then are coerced by calls for unity in these large coalitions. Can't we do better? Fortunately we can.

Radical Decentralization:
A New Beginning

So let us begin our work not in large coalitions and superstructures but in small affinity groups of friends. Within the context of our communities, the radical decentralization of work, projects, and responsibility strengthens the ability of anarchist groups to thrive and do work which best suits their particular skills and interests. We reject ineffective, tyrannical superstructures as the only means to get work done. We can do things by strengthening and supporting existing affinity groups and collectives. Why not be as critical of the need for large federations, coalitions, and other superstructures as we are of the state, religion, bureaucracies, and corporations? While no one strategy should be held eternally superior to all others, our recent successes have defied the belief that we must be part of some giant organization to get anything done. Take to heart the thousands of DIY projects being done around the world, outside of superstructures. We can come to meetings as equals and work based on our passions and ideals, and then find others with whom we share these ideals. Together we can protect our autonomy and continue to fight for liberty, trust, and true solidarity.

The DIY Metropolis:
Anarchist Models of the City

> *"It may be romantic to search for the salves of society's
> ills in slow-moving rustic surroundings, or among
> innocent unspoiled provincials, but it is a waste of
> time. Does anyone suppose that in real life, answers
> to any of the great questions that worry us today are
> going to come out of homogenous settlements?"*
> —*Jane Jacobs*

Many anarchists, along with at least half of the World's population, live in cities. Realistically, many anarchists organize in cities, work in cities, make love in cities-and love our cities. Yet there is little real analysis of what an anti-authoritarian city would be like, if such a thing is even possible, and how it might function. Many anarchists believe that cities are inherently hierarchical and thus must be completely done away with, yet they give little thought to how relocating billions of people could be accomplished without coercive hierarchies, or what impact this massive exodus would have on the rural countryside.

Others, like Murray Bookchin and his municipalitarian devotees, believe that hamlets modeled on the medieval town—or worse, a model based on the slave-holding ancient Greek cities—would provide the optimum anarchist habitat. This concept of small communities has been revisited numerous times throughout the history of anarchist thought. These partisans of small town models wish to control the size and character of the city to create a dollhouse urban space with discrete sectors and compartmentalized positions. Similar ideas have already been put into practice by Ebenezer Howard in *England's Garden Cities*, or more recently with the new-urbanism model. They have typically resulted in sterile, segregated, homogenous, pseudo-urban environments such as Celebration, Florida and Kentlands, Maryland.

While critiques of the pastoralists, municipalitarians, primitivists, Fourierists, and others are often correct in their particulars, they miss the point of why over half the world population is attracted to urban spaces. They miss the dynamic life of the city and the chaotic nature of urban existence that creates not only problems but also new forms of experiences. They overlook the possibility, the excitement and the freedom of living in the city. Even if some anarchists have written off the city, half of the world has not.

In the last two centuries, discussion about the future of cities has been dominated by specialists who implicitly hated cities. A number of urban and political theorists (from all over the political spectrum) have re-envisioned the city by neutralizing it. Le Corbusier's vision of a clean, disease-free, perfectly regulated urban environment, Lenin's dream of an industrial cooperative metropolis where workers would live communally next to their work in a drab and functional style, and Hitler and Albert Speer's plan for Berlin as an ethnically cleansed, perfectly obedient capital are not the same thing; but the distinc-

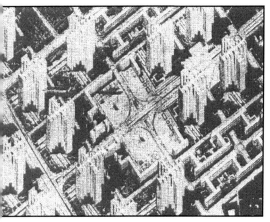

tions are not as vast as one might think. Pierre Charles L'Enfant, the planner of Washington D.C., said that the design of the capitol with such regular plans might look good on paper but on the ground they become "tiresome and insipid." Even 19th-century anarchist reformers like Charles Fourier were control ad-

dicts, even if they had some fun fantasies. Utopian city planning has imagined itself to be a sublime engine of social change: by changing the physical conditions of an imperfect thing, a city, they can make perfect people. Their paper theories have turned some of the greatest cities in the world into concrete nightmares. They refuse to address the problem of power because no one can plan or design single-handedly without accepting a position of power. Hierarchical authority and architectural authority are one and the same, and should repulse any city-loving anarchist and anarchy-loving urbanites alike.

There has been precious little written by anarchists about alternatives to the hierarchy of cities. There are a few books and decent articles written on North American and European squatters, but they are insufficient. We believe that there are more anarchist urban models, innovative and tested, that exist already in unlikely places. These are the shanties on the fringes of our largest and most dynamic urban centers.

The city is already being remade in non-hierarchical ways, not by legions of urban planners or political theorists, or even by handfuls of squatters, but by millions of everyday men and women of the Global South. Catalyzed by necessity and desire, a do-it-yourself ethic has grown up in the world's largest and most impoverished metropolitan centers. The residents of these shantytowns—*favelas* or *borgate* as they are variously called—are among the world's fastest-growing

populations. A UN global report on human settlements in 1986 pointed out that between a third to more than half of residents of most large cities in developing countries live in these types of informal settlements. We have much to learn from these organically organized models of urban living that already exist.

While it is true that the estimated one billion folks living in informal settlements are besieged by a number of life-threatening problems such as poor sanitation, lack of health care, inadequate access to basic resources, and poor nutrition, most of these problems are due to the crushing poverty that is inflicted on them by the neoliberal policies of the "developed" World. Despite these nearly insurmountable economic and political obstacles, more and more people voluntarily choose to rebuild the world's cities. What is even more impressive is that they are using many of the principles that anarchists espouse, including voluntary association, decentralization, sustainability, direct democracy, mutual aid, gift exchange, and the do-it-yourself ethic.

They have done this while embracing an organic and chaotic development that in many places has led to effective political activism and active resistance against the powers of the State and capitalism.

Our information comes from a variety of sources including NGO reports, anthropologists, urban planners, political activists, our own visits to these places, and most importantly, the people living in shanties themselves. The myth that shanties are teeming, dangerous, and depraved places where people live no better than overcrowded and caged animals simply does not hold up to the experiences of the researchers and the people living in these places. Let's delve deep into the alleys of the favelas and enter their DIY homes; we'll see another way to re-envision the city-one that looks like anarchy.

Voluntary Association

The most enduring myth of the shantytown is that its inhabitants are forced to live there due to economic need. While it is true that

families move to shantytowns in the hope of improving their economic status, for many this is not the only reason, or even the primary reason. Anthropologists in Lima's major borgatas found that people chose to live in shantytowns because they were bored with their small rural villages and sought an escape from the culturally and socially limiting traditions of highland life. A similar sentiment was echoed among shanty-dwellers in Ghana, who claimed that there were more opportunities to escape the arranged marriages, poor education, and limited career choices of the hinterlands. The Roma (Gypsies) in Bulgaria moved from rural areas to shantytowns in the major cities to avoid the often violent provincial prejudices of their rural neighbors. Or as one squatter in a shantytown outside Hong Kong said, "There is more liberty in the city. I can be myself."

People are not flocking to the cities solely for economic reasons: there is actually freedom living in the city, the possibility for individuals to reinvent themselves. In large cities there is often a cultural tolerance that does not exist in small towns, rural areas, or suburbs for that matter. Some come together in cities in large enough groups to provide security. Others flock to the density of the city for economic or educational opportunities. Assuming that shanty-dwellers are simply passive victims of economic pres-

sures would be an oversimplification, and in most cases just wrong. Shanty dwellers are often active agents in choosing to leave the rural hinterlands for a variety of reasons, and coming together in informal settlements to create a better world. Their reasons for leaving are not much different than those of anarchists in the United States today who are fleeing the deadening suburbs and small towns of their youth to congregate in squats or cheap apartments in the poor and forgotten neighborhoods of our larger cities.

Decentralization

There are many aspects of decentralization in informal settlements. Basic urban infrastructure and services are decentralized, undoubtedly due to shanties being excluded from centralized services, but for other reasons as well. Limited resources, smallness of scale, self-organization, and a desire for direct participation and control are among the reasons shanty communities embrace decentralization. Despite their lack of resources many of these decentralized services prove more effective than centralized models.

For example, the use of communal minivans in shanties in southern Istanbul is very popular. The vans run more regularly and are safer than their centralized commercial counterparts. Decentralized wells in the shanty-ghettos of Bolivia have proven so successful at providing water for inhabitants that the high and mighty United Nations planners have decided to research this model for replication in other poor regions.

Even education and childcare are often decentralized. In Lima, decentralized education is provided by "roaming" teachers who move from one tiny neighborhood school to another-sometimes up  to four schools in a single day. These teachers build relationships with various schools and agree on compensation for their services. It isn't uncommon for a small neighborhood school to get four or five teachers with substantial college education and experience who roam in and out in the course of a single school day. Without this arrangement it would be impossible for a single tiny school to hire permanent staff of such caliber. Childcare in most shantytowns, where many mothers work, is also decentralized. People (men, women, older siblings, the elderly and handicapped) not at work will take on the task of caring for the children of working parents. This allows children to have a much larger social network than in a traditional Western-style daycare. A researcher for the Cooperative Housing Foundation found that children in a shanty outside of Bogota created lasting bonds with as many as twenty-five different adults outside their families in a week, through rotating informal daycare.

Sustainability

When policy wonks, United Nations representatives on urban issues, or other specialists talk about population and city growth, they usually refer to the horrors of ever-growing shantytowns in "developing" countries. These so-called experts have succeeded in creating the image of the informal settlement as an unstable, exploding hellhole perpetually on the brink of self-destruction. While life in these settlements is full of hardships, the idea that they are all unstable, untenable, and ready to burst is simply not true. There are settlements that have appeared overnight and there are settlements that are transitory, but this is certainly not the case for all settlements. Informal settlements, such as the ones in Rio de Janeiro or Mexico City, are becoming less and less transitory. Many have been around for a long time—for centuries, in Brazil—and they have endured despite poverty, population growth, and government repression. The nature of informal settlements around the world has been changing from temporary and transitional to permanent and sustainable.

Despite the fact most shanties are located in poor sites ill suited for human living—in landfills, dumps, erosion zones, flood zones, and toxic waste areas—they have endured. Moreover, in many places their inhabitants have significantly improved the environment while creating a more livable community for themselves. In Turkey, the residents of shanties have actually protected the surround-

ing countryside from erosion by planting and tending communal olive trees. These trees, with their extensive root systems, have been more useful than the concrete jerseys used by the city government. In two of the largest and most politically active shanties in Mexico City, shanty-dwellers developed (along with students from nearby universities) an innovative way to protect the diminishing green-belt around Mexico City. The Ecologica Productiva Movement argued that by utilizing the decentralized and creative aspects of the shanties, Mexico City's endangered "green-belt" could be transformed into a thriving and diverse biological preserve while providing economic opportunities for the local inhabitants. The plan emphasized sustainable technology (like solar powered outhouses that convert organic waste into highly desirable fertilizer) and communal management of natural resources—not surprisingly, the Mexican authorities scuttled the plan. Regardless of their unpopularity with the government, these ideas are now appearing in other countries in Latin America and Africa with great initial successes.

In general, informal settlements have no redundant buildings, no excesses in living space or style—and total recycling is a way of survival. Recent research in Mexico City and Hong Kong showed that the average shanty resident produces half of one percent of the waste an average city dweller does. In addition, most large cities in the developing world have no formalized recycling program, and thus shanty residents play an important role in recycling and reducing the annual waste of these metropolises. Since both public spaces and residences are multi-use, nothing remains fallow. Even though shanties are incredibly dense, they often have more public space than some urban neighborhoods in the "developed" world. They have shown how ordinary folks have reclaimed public space at the same time as making new areas that can be used for both private and public events.

Direct Democracy

Shanty residents are always politically marginalized, and are commonly victims of repression by the State. Voting is low in shanties but

 residents make up for it in creative grassroots actions. Shanties have been laboratories for spatial and social organization and political experimentation. The most successful shanties share a commitment to direct democracy in its various forms. These successes range from building more schools to stealing access to state-owned utilities.

For direct democracy to work in a shanty, the residents need access to information about the political scene. Shanty residents are innovative in dealing with this need. For example, despite the high illiteracy rates, nearly every Mexican shantytown has at least one do-it-yourself newsletter, which is read aloud in public spaces. A shanty outside Katmandu puts out a regular comic book illustrating the current political situation in their communities and the country.

Shanty communities have utilized diverse tactics to achieve their political goals. The Ecologica Productiva Movement of Mexico City used large marches as well as coalitions with university students, environmentalists, and international non-profits to put pressure on the government for greater autonomy and the rights to their homes. Informal settlements outside Hong Kong used high profile occupations of government buildings in order to secure access to basic

utilities. The residents of a Katmandu shanty collected and dumped all of their garbage in the central market place thus forcing the government to resume waste removal in their communities. All of these actions were accomplished without formal, representational organizations being involved. In Mexico City, the attempt at forming such an organization actually led to the downfall of the Ecologica Productiva Movement and resulted in the destruction of the participating informal settlements. What happened in Mexico City has been replicated in US communities. When we try to become "legal," whether it is getting deeds for our squats or permits for our marches, we run the risk of making the same fatal mistake as the Mexico City squatters.

Mutual Aid and Gift Exchange

One of the most obvious aspects of shanties is their crushing poverty. Shanties have few internal resources and their access to the city's wealth is tenuous and exploitative at best. This has led creative shanty residents to develop and implement a number of alternative economic models to ensure their survival. Obviously theft, parasitism, and informal economies can be found in nearly every shantytown

APOYEMOS LA LUCHA DEL AJUSCO

RECHAZO A LOS DESALOJOS O REHUBICACIONES RESPETO A LA POSESIÓN Y A LOS DERECHOS DE LOS COLONOS

BELVEDERE, 2 DE OCTUBRE Y BOSQUES

and poor inner city neighborhood but these are not the primary ways they obtain needed resources.

Mutual aid is an important aspect of every successful shantytown and distinguishes them from bleak inner city neighborhoods. From building shelters, sharing tools, and working on communal gardens to providing each other rides to and from work, needs are met using mutual aid. Gift-giving is also important. One anthropologist who spent five years living in a settlement in Ghana estimated that almost one-third of all resources were given away. Gift giving is an important way to reinforce friendships and build new social networks. It also provides a safety net for those unable to work. Rotating credit and debt are also another common feature of shantytowns. Interest-free debt is a way for shanty inhabitants to weather the inherent instability in their employment. Obtaining large amounts of capital is often done informally through a lottery system. Families and

individuals put money into a common kitty that is given to one participant each month. This allows that person to have enough resources to
make a major purchase such as building supplies, or start a business.

Accumulation of wealth is not prized in a shanty, nor is it practical—ownership occurs by use or occupancy. It is safer to give your
resources away and widen your social net than to hoard resources.
Anarchists can take a lesson from this generosity in our conferences,
demonstrations, and gatherings.

Social and Spatial Organization

"The street is the river of life."

In informal settlements the organization and creation of space,
the way houses are arranged and linked together, the width and
direction of streets, and the formation of public spaces stems directly
from the way residents are organized socially. This organization is
based on affinity. Affinity can be fostered by a variety of forces such
as geography, familial ties and alliances, friendships, and professional bonds, as well as political and cultural associations.

Affinity fosters an emphasis on the neighborhood as a whole. In
contrast to the traditional Western city dweller, significant time and
resources are spent sustaining and increas-
ing social ties. In Ghanian shanties, most of
a family's annual economic resources are
spent on communal activities like feast days,
weddings, parties, and baptisms. In Lima,
men spend half the day in large groups socializing, while women spend even more of
their day hanging out in such groups. Children in almost all informal
settlements spend most of their waking hours in large mixed groups
of adults and children.

Socializing is key to physical, political, and economic survival inside shanty communities. Due to the widespread prejudice against

residents in shanty-towns, and their need to enter hostile areas for employment, they need the extended network to protect them against attacks from outsiders. They also need cohesive social networks to protect themselves physically from regularly occurring assaults in the shanty districts by police, army, paramilitary, and other governmental agencies. Social networks provide the glue that holds temporary coalitions of squatters together to launch large-scale political campaigns, and make them resistant to both co-optation and divisive tactics by authorities. These alliances are also effective in controlling

disruptive forces inside the settlement. The use of gossip, shunning, and other social controls limits destructive behavior in tightly knit neighborhoods.

Individuals are dependent on a complex and extensive web of economic relationships. These webs are expanded and reinforced by friendships and other forms of togetherness. For example, it would be impossible for individual families to obtain the materials and supply all the labor needed to build adequate shelter without the aid of these social networks. Even education, health care, and basic utilities are dependent on informal social relationships.

The constant need for socialization influences the way spaces are used. Informal settlements emphasize public spaces, often by redefining them. Boundaries between the public and private, so beloved by urbanists, are blurred, and sometimes nonexistent in these communities.

Most spaces accommodate a variety of uses—a street can be the place for a soccer game, vending, hanging out, showing off, and a transportation corridor all at the same time. A private home is not just a living space but also a retail shop, daycare center, and a community-gathering place. Furthermore, space within the house is not specialized the way Western living space is. In the course of a day, a single room may be used as a bedroom, a sitting room, a dining room, a children's room, and a place of work—sometimes all at once. All of this reinforces the power of socialization in these types of communities.

The same principles of socialization can be applied to our infoshops, autonomous zones, and convergences. We must be willing to take the time and make the space for meaningful socialization.

Do-It-Yourself Architecture

The do-it-yourself ethic is more than a strategic way to use limited resources; it also has a number of important advantages over commercial and professional enterprises. Do-it-yourself creates greater participation than the consumer relationship of professional encounters. It also allows individuals to customize their projects to their desires and skills, putting a premium on skill-sharing, as opposed to the skill-hoarding so prevalent among experts. Shared work outside the traditional capitalist model creates meaningful relationships among participants. Communal projects like barn-raising have traditionally been very important in maintaining strong social ties inside a community. The do-it-yourself ethic puts a premium on the indigenous: skills, resources, and participants. Perhaps most importantly, it empowers individuals and creates a genuine shared investment in the community. These projects flourish in every shanty community ranging from complicated sanitation systems to simple soccer fields. The most common project is architecture: building homes and other structures. In the capitalist world, the dominion of architects, building inspectors, engineers, and other experts is so complete that we can hardly imagine people constructing their own homes. The experts today have managed to obscure the skills. Most shanty homes are never "finished;" the building form is flexible, rooms are constantly being added as need. Building one's home is a work-in-progress, a never-ending project.

The use of informal structures is usually based on need. Informal settlement inhabitants "own" a structure when they occupy it, and when they put work and effort into improving it, similar to Western style squats. In most shanty towns there are no empty or unused houses: when a family moves out of a structure, another one moves in.

> *"The city air makes you free!"*
> *—Medieval saying*

We are not arguing that shanty communities are perfect or even that all shanties exhibit all the above anarchistic qualities. Instead,

we feel that shanty communities provide real life and death models of how we can remake and reclaim the city. We can do this without giving up our anarchist ideals. The shanties are an enormous on-going social experiment. They are a test of the effectiveness of voluntary association, decentralization, sustainability, direct democracy, mutual aid and the do-it-yourself ethic in the most difficult urban environments. If they can do it, so can we!

Let's acknowledge and celebrate the attraction cities have on our imagination and our desire for liberty and community. Unlike our predecessors, the last thing we want is to control and regulate the city, starving it of its organic nature and stripping it of its spontaneity—we want the city to be *out of control*. We are not creating the paper cities of theorists but invoking what millions of others have already done. We are suggesting an informal approach to cities and settlements: stripping away the need for highly specialized professionals and replacing them with a community of shared skills. We replace developers, landlords and land speculators with creative builders and home-occupants based not on investment, ownership, or capital but simply on occupancy.

We wish to free the city to shape itself based on the needs of its inhabitants and on a sustainable relationship with the surrounding ecosystem. We need cities that are alive and evolving, not a pre-planned nightmare of grids, cloverleafs, and dismal subdivisions. We reject the atomization of the suburb, apartment complex, and rural shack, and embrace teeming, complex anarchist communities. We have to be confident enough in ourselves and our neighbors to allow chaos to return to the cities—bringing new problems to be solved and creating new experiences not available anywhere other than the living city.

No City Will Be Safe From Anarchy!

The Inefficient Utopia:
Or How Consensus Will Change the
World

Over and over again, anarchists have been critiqued, arrested, and killed by "fellow-travelers" on the road to revolution because we were deemed inefficient. Trotsky complained to his pal Lenin that the anarchists in charge of the railways were "...inefficient devils. Their lack of punctuality will derail our revolution." Lenin agreed, and in 1919, the anarchist Northern Rail Headquarters was stormed by the Red Guard and the anarchists were "expelled from their duties." Charges of inefficiency were not only a matter of losing jobs for anarchists, but an excuse for the authorities to murder them. Even today, anarchist principles are condemned roundly by those on the Left as simply not efficient enough. We are derided because we would rather be opening a squat or cooking big meals for the hungry than selling newspapers. These criticisms from the larger activist scene have had scurrilous effects. More disturbing than these outside attacks, anarchists have begun to internalize and repeat this criticism. Some have attempted to gain efficiency with such means as officers, federations, and voting. All of this is done to scare away the hobgoblin of inefficiency that has dogged anarchism for so long.

Don't believe the hype.

Instead, rejoice in inefficiency and rightfully reject the idol-worship of the Ford Factory of political change. Efficiency is the hallmark of modern life in North America: from fast food drive-ins to well-regulated police states. Efficiency is the coin of the realm for soulless structures like the International Monetary Fund and the earth destroying agribusiness industry. The desire to "do more in less time" is not a neutral force in our culture; it is the handmaiden of miserable experts, specialists, and leaders.

Not everyone has rushed to become efficient. Something else exists on the periphery—an inefficient utopia, a culture of consensus, collectives, and do-it-yourself ethics. A place where time is not bought, sold, or leased, and no clock is the final arbiter of our worth. For many people in North America, the problem is not just poverty but lack of time to do the things that are actually meaningful. This is not a symptom of personal failures but the consequence of a time-obsessed society. Today desire for efficiency springs from the scarcity model which is the foundation of capitalism. Time is seen as a limited resource when we get caught up in meaningless jobs, mass-produced entertainment, and—the common complaint of activists—tedious meetings. So let's make the most of our time!

In our politics and projects, anarchists have rightly sought to find meaning in the journey, not merely in the intended destinations. Inefficiency allows us the opportunity to seek out our affinities and engage in meaningful work without the sands of time burying our ideals. Despite the advice of high school counselors and computer graded exams, it takes time to know what you really want to do with your life.

In the efficient dystopia that is North America, "Time is Money." Yet there is never enough time or money for what we really need. Our communities of resistance have rightly placed a great deal of emphasis on exchanging skills and knowledge through do-it-yourself workshops, trainings, rendezvous, and convergences. As opposed to the corporate or academic models, DIY skill sharing requires time-consuming encounters that create genuine relationships based on friendship and mutual trust. In the pursuit of efficiency, meaningful relationships like these are replaced by professionalization and reliance on specialists. Do we really need "professional" facilitators to run our meetings? In contrast to skill-sharing, professionalized relationships leave all parties cold and lacking, whether the transaction involves having your car repaired or receiving vital health care. Both the consumer and specialist are cheating themselves of the

opportunity to learn new skills and befriend new people. The specialist becomes trapped in doing what she is good at or specialized in, and rarely what she actually wants to do.

Equally trapped, the consumer loses her own autonomy when relationships are reduced to efficient monetary exchanges. This alienated consumer works against her own interests; she knows little about who she is bankrolling. She may be saving her money in a bank that is lending it to the real-estate gentrifiers that are destroying her local neighborhood and raising her rent. Often we repeat these capitalistic interactions in our communities of resistance, giving our time and money to organizations we know almost nothing about. A rogue member of the Curious George Brigade was recently hit up for a donation by a volunteer of the giant anti-war coalition who was toting around a giant garbage bag, in the streets, during the actual demonstration! When asked where that big bag of money would actually wind up, the volunteer shrugged her shoulders and candidly answered, "You know, to be honest, I don't know. I just follow directions." Needless to say, we wound up donating our money to the bail fund instead. In life and activism, we should know who we are working with; otherwise voluntary association is just a slogan. All of this takes time.

Inefficiency rots away the ideological foundations of the modern capitalist State. Workers know that politically motivated inefficiency (e.g. work slowdowns) is an important tool to gain power in the workplace. Imagine extending the work-slowdown to the political process and to every facet of society. Political inefficiency can be an important tool for checking authoritarian tendencies in larger groups. For

example, at an impersonal, business-like meeting, you can reject a predetermined plan of action by organizers and demand time and a venue to discuss real alternatives. Too many times activists have been strong-armed into poorly made, myopic plans created by tiny groups and self-appointed leaders. It is necessary to reject prepackaged politics the same way we reject prepackaged food in favor of a home cooked meal made with friends.

Political Inefficiency

Consensus may take more time than voting, but then voting is not as time-efficient as totalitarianism. What little is gained in efficiency is usually at the cost of genuine participation and autonomy. At its very core, consensus demands participation and input from the entire community. In an environment of mutual trust, consensus is one of the few decision-making models that truly rejects authority while protecting the autonomy of individuals and small groups. When consensus works, everyone can participate and all desires are taken into account. And while there is no magic formula for creating a good meeting or social interaction, we should never sacrifice our ideals and politics for false unity. We talk of maintaining biodiversity and ethnic diversity, but what about political and tactical diversity? When the voice of every minority faction, or individual is sacrificed in the name of efficiency the horizon of our politics shrinks. When people are sidelined, we all lose out. Never confuse efficiency with effectiveness.

Inefficient Organization

Affinity groups (AGs) tend to be less efficient than armies, hierarchical organizations, and other mass-based organizational models. By their very structure, AGs take every individual's opinion seriously. This is a much less efficient principle of organization than a party whose leaders make decisions unilaterally. What AGs lack in size, efficiency and mobilization of resources, they more than make up for in participation, genuine experiences, and solidarity. The dinosaurs on the Left

tell us that we must get armies, seize government power, and most of all, be state-like in order to "win." Why should we let the State set the terms of our resistance anyway? Anarchists can come up with more flexible strategies. Our networks gladly lack a precise platform of principles and unceasing meetings. Instead, we have irregular gatherings, rendezvous for specific projects, multiple skills, solid friendships, and limitless ambitions unconstrained by organizational hierarchies. Through these networks of trust, people can feel comfortable with the most outrageous of actions while receiving the care and warmth needed to carry on. They may not be ageless and permanent, but these models rarely outlive their usefulness, unlike formal parties and other efficient organizations which lumber on into irrelevancy.

We don't need to preplan every contingency in an attempt to be superhumanly efficient. Anarchists take care of each other and our friends. A group of bands get together to hold a benefit show for a local group of strikers and move on after the money is given to those in need. These relationships can be mutually beneficial, perhaps those musicians might need the strikers to help defend their squat next week! This is in stark contrast to many organizations that collect monthly dues to hide away in war-chests waiting for the "right time" to spend it. Inefficient organizations allow each individual to express themselves to the fullest of their abilities in cooperation with others, unlike large groups where most people are just another face

One of the most inefficient utopias I have ever seen was that of a humble Zapatista village in the mountains of southeastern Mexico. I kid you not; the entire village sits down and takes days to make a single decision! Everyone gets a chance to hear and be heard and some questions take eons, but everyone is patient and respectful. Things actually get done. It is as if time was suddenly transformed from the ticking of a Newtonian clock to something that revolved around ordinary folks.

Mexican peasants, under the constant threat of government extermination, take time to decide everything by consensus. It isn't strange to them to discuss problems and issues until everyone can agree on a decision. I hope to live in a society where we can take time to show each other how we all really do matter. Instead of reaching only for meetings with thousands of people in the US, we can replicate this process with small groups of friends. Consensus is not a two-hour meeting with everything decided beforehand, it is the time spent to discuss and understand issues of real importance, a tactical method for building networks that are stronger than anything hierarchy could ever offer. With enough time, we will accomplish things with "villages" of hundreds, even thousands. This will produce consensus that doesn't seek to impose uniformity but foster and create alliances which celebrate differences. I can only imagine the possibilities.

—Regina de Bray,
anarchist adventurer and professional amateur

in the crowd. Our networks do not need to have officers, a manifesto, or necessarily even a name. Can such networks pose a significant alternative to the established political system? Just a few years ago the military's pet think tank RAND Corp. wrote this about the unpermitted, unscripted elements of the N30 demos in Seattle:

"Anarchists, using extremely good modern communications, including live internet feeds, were able to execute simultaneous actions by means of pulsing and swarming tactics coordinated by networked and leaderless 'affinity groups.' It became an example of the challenges that hierarchical organizations face when confronting networked adversaries with faster reaction cycles. This loosely organized coalition, embracing network organization and tactics, frustrated police efforts to gain the situational awareness needed to combat the seemingly chaotic Seattle disturbances."

Inefficient Propaganda

The demand for quality experiences is an important propaganda tool in a society that produces meaningless quantity: a billion television channels with nothing on. One of the challenges we face is to transform a society of passive consumers into active and creative participants in their own futures, by any means necessary.

Opening the flows of communication is key to creating anarchy. Graffiti, zines, pirate radio, subvertisements, billboard defacements, and websites may not reach the large audiences of mass media but their impact is often more lasting on both the producers and the audience. As more people take control of "the message," more voices are heard. This decentralization of message and medium creates a culture of propagandists ruthlessly pirating and creating information to form their own messages. The difference between consumer and producer shrinks when everyone can have their voice heard. This is the central concept behind the Independent Media Centers. Eventually the entire dichotomy breaks down as media skills are learned and shared. It's actually more impressive to see thousands of diverse voices each expressing a unique perspective on their current situation than the same mass-produced issue-of-the-week signs that are given away by organizers at every large march.

Anarchists seek not only to increase their audiences but also to increase the diversity of mediums and people who have the ability to reach audiences. By creating a culture of propagandists skilled in getting their messages across, our communication becomes simultaneously more honest and more complex. The tricks used by capitalist advertisements to fool us into buying their newest product can be transformed into weapons in our hands for dismantling this system. A sexist billboard selling Coors is changed into a demand for veganism, perplexing passing motorists. Books of propaganda become more meaningful when their pages get ripped out, photocopied, stolen, reinterpreted, edited, and passed on.

Tactical Inefficiency

"You are a bunch of anti-organizationalists, and we are fighting to win" is a recent critique against those who share some of our tactics in the activist community. Activists who pursue efficiency would have us believe that anarchist principles may be fine for an ideal world or even after the comfortably far off Revolution, but for now they are unpractical, selfish, and dangerous. These activists march smugly under the faded banners of political discipline, efficiency, and sensibility. What is so ironic is that these marching groups are often the least effective groups on the streets, at least as far as social and political change is concerned. Thirty-odd years of marching around with signs in America has made little progress against the onslaught of capitalist and state power. Maybe it's time to try something different? It certainly won't be easy. Our enemies are unified enough to throw major obstacles in our way. They have armies, media, money, resources, jails, religions, and countless other tools at their disposal to stop any revolutionary change that risks upsetting their current positions of power. Our inefficient models are the most meaningful way of ensuring that we maximize our opportunities. Consensus allows us to use all the ideas of all participants. It is worth the time to make sure our projects have the greatest chance of success by listening to everyone's opinion and taking them seriously. We will need all of our skills, resources, and creativity to resist them, remake our own lives and society.

Only in groups where they feel valued, trusted, and secure will people be willing to take the time to present unpopular views and suggestions that will determine the outcome of a project. Responsibility ought to be based on friendship and autonomy not on a slavish following of leaders, platforms, or abstract dogmas. Each person in an affinity group must account for their actions, words, and deeds to their most trusted comrades. We reject the blame game and accusations so common in efficient groups. With each person accepting full responsibility for their actions, no one can have any more of the blame than any one else. Let's all be accountable to ourselves, so we can grow and learn from our mistakes and be buoyed by our successes. It takes time to understand people, to develop friendships and trust. It is naive to think that by proclaiming a platform or points of unity we can develop trust and solidarity with strangers. Politics should not be tied to some abstract timeline divined by leaders or musty books but to our own instincts and desires! Demand the time to think, form meaningful relationships, and enjoy the journey. For any chance at success, we must love each other more than our enemy hates us. To these ends, our inefficiency is our weapon.

IT'S ONLY A MATTER OF TIME, ANYWAY.

This Is Folk Anarchy!

What sort of anarchy have we been talking about? What threads connect this anarchy of mutinies and metropolises, that takes today what tomorrow never brings? It's folk anarchy; an anarchy created for and by ordinary people living extraordinary lives. Folk anarchy demands complete world revolution, and within the shadows of the dinosaur, it is busily creating a new world today. To help folks realize that they are capable of creating anything—this is our aim, our conspiracy, and our task.

Folk Anarchy vs. Faux Anarchy

Folk anarchy is more than a dream, it is a way to describe what we're already doing today: how our projects and passions fit together... warts and all. It is not another ideological faction too busy with theories to actually engage in anarchy but rather an evolving approach describing what our communities have already created. Even our smallest victories are far more meaningful than the dinosaurs, and sometimes even ourselves, realize. While we began this book with a vicious denunciation of the dinosaurs and all those awed by their power, who might ape their ways, it is far more valuable to concentrate on what allows anarchy to happen. After all, the dinosaurs are clearly doomed: their war-machinery has put a cloud over the future of humanity, their industrial infrastructure may well destroy our ecosystems within our lifetimes. Against a tidal wave of despair, folk anarchy provides an example of hope for a world that, upon closer inspection, may not be so doomed after all.

This approach to anarchy draws upon several basic themes, revolving around regular folks (as opposed to a mythical, singular illusion such as "The Folk"). Some disingenuous critics may be quick to point out that national socialism drew heavily on the notion of The Folk. However, we mean folk as in Woodie Guthrie's "folk music" and Zora Neal Hurston's "folk tales," not as the Nazis abused it in *Volkswagen*. Fascism requires centralization of power, thrives on hierarchy, and demands purity (whether it is ethnic or ideological). For these obvious reasons, folk anarchy is the exact opposite of fascism:

creating decentralized networks, fiercely guarding our autonomy, and celebrating diversity whether in individuals or their ideas. We refuse to relinquish the imagery of folks taking control of their own lives to past and future fascists; we are reclaiming this idea because it is meaningful and inspiring today. In a world where words can be so meaningless, anarchy is a word worth fighting for.

Folk is not a new flavor of anarchy. It is neither a prefix like *Green* Anarchy or a suffix like Anarcho-*Communism*. Folk anarchy resists orthodoxy, including anarcho-orthodoxy! Folk is not a faction, splinter group, or rebellion against another tendency. It has no color in the anarchist rainbow; it embraces the entire spectrum. This living anar-

chy is based on a web of practices that seems to thrive everywhere that the dinosaurs do not control. Folk anarchy sprouts up differently in favalehs and farms, in squats and street demos. People can embrace a folk approach to anarchy while maintaining other orientations, whether specific, newer concepts such as "tranar-

chy" or ChuckO's inclusive notion of "big tent" anarchy. Folk describes the participants (the same way the term "folk art" is used), not their particular ideologies. The only approaches that are excluded are those that slide into authoritarianism, professionalism, and elitism.

There is no singular "Folk Anarchism" and there hopefully never will be. The moment anarchy becomes capital-A Anarchism, with all the requisite platforms and narrow historical baggage, it is transformed from the activity of people into yet another stale ideology for sale on the marketplace.

Culture as a Dare

While culture can be co-opted, folk approaches to anarchy cannot. The moment something becomes co-opted, owned, and created by corporations, it is out of the hands of ordinary people and is lost. A street vendor can hawk a patch with a "circle-A" symbol, a bookstore can sell you a book of anarchist theory (we even sold you this book!) but no one can ever sell you the experience of living anarchy. You have to *do it yourself*. Capitalism can sell you a video game of a riot, but they can't sell you the feeling of running through the streets in solidarity with other people. The merchants of desire can sell you a romance novel, but they can't sell you the tender embrace of a new lover. We can never be satisfied with images, theories, manifestos, webpages, or books. Demand the real thing—anarchy in our own lives—right here and right now!

The paths that lead us from where we are right now to where we want to be are difficult, but the allies and tools we need to help us are already available. Folk anarchy is a culture of theft that enables us to steal the best of every ideology, the finest of past experiences, and creatively use them in our present struggles to create empowering experiences and lives. In these lives, we can create an activism that is truly revolutionary if we have the courage to step beyond feeble community organizing based on stereotypes, and beyond the fetishization of violence, as well as the million other dead ends that dinosaur-obsessed activists take. In our goal of spreading anarchy, there are no excuses, however convenient, for lack of action. Some people will try to dissuade us, pointing out these are not revolutionary times. There is no such thing as revolutionary times. Time does not rule us: we create the times, revolutionary or not. When we break free from our chains of routine and hierarchy, the times are revolutionary.

Capitalism teaches us that we are data blips: dots on demographic charts that are born to work, commute, consume, and eventually die. Every fiber of our bodies knows something else exists beyond this depressing cycle, and we yearn for real connections with other people. Anarchy is not just a political strategy or a collection of tactics; anarchy is a web of conscious connections that is now consciously global. Every direct and personal action of solidarity that anarchists commit builds and strengthens this web. When folks from North America travel to South America and meet with anarchists there, the web grows—just as much as it is when we meet and discuss our lives with people living down the street who have never even heard of anarchy. Those people down the street could show us a trick or two as well! However, could just living our lives to the utmost be a revolutionary strategy worth pursuing? Is revolution worth not only dying for, but living for?

Communities of Resistance Meet the Revolution of Everyday Life

> "*The everyday practical activity of the tribesmen reproduces, or perpetuates, a tribe. The reproduction is not merely physical but social as well. Through their daily activities, the tribesmen do not merely reproduce a group of human beings, they reproduce a tribe, namely a particular social form within which this group of human beings performs specific activities in a specific manner. The everyday activity of slaves reproduces slavery. If the everyday life of capitalists reproduces capitalism… what does the everyday life of anarchists create? Could it be… anarchy?*"
>
> —*Stanford Sociology professor turned ELF spokesperson*

The revolution of everyday life serves as the bedrock of our communities of resistance, and no genuine community of resistance can exist without a revolution of everyday life. The corollary to this is that if there is to be revolution, it must encourage a personal transformation of the individual folks as well as the formation of revolutionary communities.

To reach these lofty aims, we need people strong enough to re- fuse to die for ideology or personal profit, people who can not only destroy the current capitalist system and its institutions, but who will utterly prevent the creation of the next dinosaur. It is easy for pro- spective revolutionaries to fall into the trap of power after any at- tempted revolution, becoming the leaders and presidents of a new regime. The only way to prevent this retracing of the path of the dinosaurs is to break out of these habits in our everyday lives. Past attempts at revolution have shown that the abusive father, the petty bureaucrat of an obscure communist party, or the authoritarian com- mander of the revolutionary cell will all become full-fledged dicta- tors if the power becomes available to them. We suspect that the freedom-loving individual who is constantly challenging power within herself by creating revolutionary situations in every interaction is far more likely to actually dismantle power. Yet these individuals alone can only do so much. By working together in a community their poten- tial grows exponentially. The anarchist individual gains the ability to actually practice anarchy through living in these kinds of communities.

These communities are in resistance exactly because they re-chan- nel power to everybody by resisting both internal and external urges towards centralizing power. Affinity groups, decentralized networks, collectives, and consensus are all folk tools that are being used in these communities today and will be needed in the future. These are not just means to the end, they are ends of themselves. Some may call this think- ing "utopian." Just because anarchists can pull it off at a convergence or infoshop, the critics will argue, doesn't mean it's possible to create successful communities on the same principles. Yet the impossible exists all around us, if only our critics would turn off their televisions and com- puters. From indigenous women remaking their communities in Chiapas, to punks serving free food in Tompkins Square Park, to tree-sitters sharing tales at an encampment in Cascadia… we are surrounded by folk anarchy. Yes, all of these examples come from radically different environments, but who says that we must have a single utopia? Once ordinary people have reached a place where the experts told us we could never go, we'll just head for an even more impossible place!

Folk anarchy is just *keeping it real*. Let us also apply that maxim not only to politics but also to our lives. After all, what is more utopian than to wait for change until after the next election, until the federation has got just a few more members, or until the theory has been perfected? What could be more realistic than demanding revolution in our daily lives, ways of providing free food, squatted shelter, poetry to inflame the heart, and the flames needed to burn down their banks? Folk anarchy is both utopian and realistic in the finest senses of those words. Keeping it real prevents meaningless scenesterism and over-hyped revolutionary swagger that are symptoms of a lack of community where people can really express both their fears and hopes in honest communication. Such communication is the cornerstone to our communities and our lives.

Communities don't have to be temporally and spatially located to be real or meaningful. Too many people live in the same apartment building and don't even know each other. Communities can exist stretched out over vast expanses of time and distance. Think of the ever-growing number of communities built only through the internet where most members will never meet face-to-face. However, for all the vast distances of space and time that keep us separate, people still need to meet face-to-face. Folk anarchy exists when people meet and join at the same space or time, be it at social forums, mobilizations, homes, music shows, or while traveling. Communities are knit together by what is held in common—and it's definitely not just common ideals or a common platform. Communities are held together by common experiences, blood and sweat, love and battle… or not at all.

Communities aren't simply born, they also die, and this too is a source of strength. Being tied to past models leads often to a strangulation of the imagination… and we need all of our creativity. Let's build these revolutionary communities based on our particular and changing realities. We shouldn't be afraid of leaving our old communities; others will take them and make them their own just as we had inherited them from others. We are thieves in the night, taking the best of anything that we find and using it to further our own purposes, and then moving on. We are picking the locks of imagination. Anarchy is not the end, anarchy is a beginning.

The Death of Purity:
Long Live the Hybrid!

Hybrids survive when the purebreds die out. Like dinosaurs, most "pure" creatures are overspecialized at the expense of their adaptability and cannot survive as soon as their environment makes an unexpected shift. The perpetual search for theoretical and practical purity is exhausting, and in the end, self defeating. At every acrimonious conference, in every blistering email exchange, in every screeching volley of letters to the editors of anarchist magazines, it is easy to see that the ideologues among us are becoming more and more of a drag. Some of us keep attacking each other in the service of our favorite absolutist vision with the kind of venom that should be reserved for those that oppress us. Too many times it devolves the necessary debates over tactics, strategy, and focus into the kind of popularity contests, ideological shell games, and cults of personality that are so despicable in mainstream politics and the Left. Instead of advancing a narrow anarcho-orthodoxy, it is time for the search for purity to be abandoned.

Despite the best attempts of groups searching for a specific, homogenous, coherent trajectory for the American anarchist community, there is none: it is diverse, flexible, decentralized, chaotic, and adaptable. The spread of folk anarchy is simple. Individual social relationships are the foundations for hybrid networks of resistance. When someone from Virginia and someone from California meet at a conference in Florida and work together, play together, fall in love, and maintain their connection when they part ways, they are creating a network. When they visit each other and bring friends, coordinate their next travels and aid each other along the way, the only worldwide-web that matters is built and strengthened. Tomorrow, they may be fighting cops next to each other, planting gardens for community supported agriculture, or working in collective spaces.

These networks begin with individuals working together, then quickly mutate into hybrid communities that can have an impact on our everyday lives. These tangible and reciprocal relationships between local, regional, and global struggles have been very clearly articulated by groups like the Zapatistas and others. Realizing how global oppressions are networked and to what maniacal ends our enemies will go to maintain their power, we realize our resistance must even be more powerful and more complex.

For example, the indigenous U'wa's threat to commit mass suicide in Colombia mobilized activists in the US and Europe ranging from unemployed Earth First!ers to well-endowed liberals to put pressure on Occidental Petroleum. Through a diversity of tactics, including boycotts and invading their stockholder meetings, these pressures forced the company to withdraw their oil bid on the U'wa land. We have learned that any resistance to global oppressions must be met with a resistance that is just as intertwined and complex, if not more. For these reasons, no single platform or party line will be meaningful and effective for all our communities of resistance.

Successful networks are created through many unexpected channels. We exchange information through Indymedia, anarchist periodicals, do-it-yourself videos, books, discussion groups, workshops, and through the experiences of our daily lives. We are youth, wimmin, members of ethnic minority groups, queers, artists, agitators, students, teachers, and street rebels. Everyone and anyone can participate in global resistance, and it is only through the diversity of our struggles that we begin to answer to the tough questions that face us.

Do-it-Yourself Politics

"Do it, do it, do it, don't stop, don't stop, don't stop."
—Anarchist folk chant from Florida, late 1990s.

Doing-it-yourself is valuable for its own sake, not just because you don't have the money to pay a specialist to do it for you. Transposed against mass culture, do-it-yourself is a wildly successful strategy and philosophy. For folk anarchists, it levels the playing field between those with different material resources, helps us share our skills to become less dependent on any one individual, and helps us create cultures of resistance.

The road to totalitarianism is paved with good intentions. As every corporate CEO knows, actually possessing steady supplies of resources and money is the clearest and shortest path to authority. By necessity do-it-yourself is the inverse: it involves us ordinary folks sharing what resources, skills, and creativity we have to get extraordinary things done.

This isn't merely a retread of the artisan vs. mass-production argument. Our anarchies must strive to be inclusive enough to allow *anybody* to have at least the option of learning to do *everything*. Isn't it strange that people who gladly endorse do-it-yourself for repairing bicycles and making music suddenly start quoting dead theorists or blindly begin copying the State and other dinosaurs when it comes to politics? We need the courage to do politics ourselves!

In the Belly of the Beast

Burning the American flag has become something of
an initiation rite for young radicals. Across the world
the message of "Yankee Go Home" is clear, but in the
borders of this fat nation, burning our own flag has
a more ominous set of possibilities. I wonder what
phoenix will rise from the ashes of the red, white,
and blue turned black in fire?
—journal entry of black bloc participant,
Bush's crashed inauguration 2000.

Specific models and solutions are needed for different regions and contexts. Folk anarchy is as old as resistance to any form of domination, and so is as much a part of American history as violence and apple pie. Right now, we're beginning to see the conscious articulation of many of these unconscious principles in anarchist communities in North America. We draw on and are inspired by anarchist agitation in the last century as well as successful models that are not traditionally anarchist, whether they are egalitarian shantytowns in South Asia, Zapatismo in Chiapas, mutinies on the battlefield, neighborhood committees in Argentina, nomadic peoples, and so on. All struggles are born out of their particular location, set of circumstances, raw materials, and local ideas. Our struggles in the United States are converging with global struggles to create a folk anarchy that knows no borders or limits. Anarchy doesn't mean a singular revolution, but thousands of revolutions.

Privileged people in the First World need to contemplate our role and actions in these global struggles. We are the children in the giant fortress, some of us the children of slaves and others of the masters, peering over the wall into a world despoiled and wrecked for the benefit of the lords of the castle. Will we mutiny against our mad captains or continue to fight among ourselves for the scraps? We must decide, as the workers, artisans, beggars, and thieves contained and protected behind the walls of Fortress America, what our next move will be and how can work with our friends in the lands outside the castle. Throughout the world people are struggling for folk anarchy—to live their lives as they see fit. When anarchists in the United States get our act together to create some real anarchy, there will be more hope for everyone else in the world.

Is it possible for black flowers to grow in the acrid belly of the beast? The promises of the United States offer us no refuge or grounding: the hollow promises of the American dream will never fill our bellies with food or fire. Yet we are growing, outside the spotlight of mass media. Our current communities of resistance are woefully imperfect yet always changing, patched together bits of older and more exotic cultures of resistance. The totems of the traveler—the patches, the bicycles, the bagels—are not much on the surface but they are a challenge to monoculture and the rule of dinosaurs. Some anarchists in the US reject their past outright, preferring to live in the shadows of revolutionary Spain, or in a Stone Age before technology. Yet many of us have rejected defeatism and have begun to pick up the broken fragments and lost toys. Using whatever is at hand, anarchy can create a refuge for refugees from the world of the dinosaurs. From the punk to the housewife, the immigrant to the college dropout, we all want something more than our limited options of subcultures—and our best chance is to make something new together. So let's not just create another refuge from the dinosaurs, but a revolution that will destroy them. Our ability to put the heat on the master dinosaurs of America will relieve immense pressures globally and… who knows what next?

If the American culture of movies, shopping malls, and soft drinks cannot inspire us, there are other Americas that can: Americas of renegades and prisoners, of dreamers and outsiders. Something can be salvaged from the twisted wreck of the "democratic spirit" celebrated by Walt Whitman, something subverted from the sense that each person has worth and dignity, a spirit that can be sustained on self-reliance and initiative. These Americas are Americas of the alienated and the marginalized: indigenous warriors, the freedom fighters of civil rights, the miners rebelling in the Appalachian Mountains. America's past is full of revolutionary hybrids; our lists could stretch infinitely onwards towards undiscovered past or future. This monolith of a rich and plump America must be destroyed to make room for many Americas. A folk anarchist culture is rising in the periphery of America and can grow in the fertile ground that lies beneath the concrete of the great American wasteland.

Anyone struggling today—living the hard life and fighting the even harder fight—is a friend even if he or she can never share a single meal with us or speak our language. The anarchists of America, with our influences as wide as our prairies and dreams that could light those prairies on fire, have no single vision of the future. In the US, where people can make entire meals on discarded food, live in abandoned buildings, and travel on the secret paths of lost highways and railroads, we are immensely privileged. We cannot ignore this. So the question is how globally American anarchists can utilize this privilege to bolster anarchy everywhere. This challenge must give rise to immense love, unending possibilities, and global solidarity: a future immense enough for everyone.

Go Tell Your Folks

So this book is almost done. As you can see, only a few thin pages are left until the end. Any final word on folk anarchy is necessarily anti-climatic; one collective can't say it all. Your mind may be wondering, "What was all this about?" Or you may wonder, "How is folk anarchy any different than just plain old anarchy?" If these are your questions, we will admit now these final pages will undoubtedly leave you unfulfilled. Perhaps your conception of anarchy is exactly what we mean when we say "folk anarchy," or more likely only some of these ideas make sense for your life. There are no easy-to-digest definitions or pithy 10 steps to liberation. What we want to share instead is how these folk approaches can work, how they are working, and how we all can keep the spirit of folk anarchy alive in our projects.

Folk anarchists exist today beneath the surface of the global capitalist empire. Folk anarchy is shaped by individuals who consciously reject easy ideologies, allow chaos to form their projects, and rely on whatever and whomever is at hand. Of course, something so eclectic by its nature will defy any singular definitions. Here's the open secret of folk anarchy: anarchy is everywhere! Folk anarchy is what people are doing today all over the world, in places all over

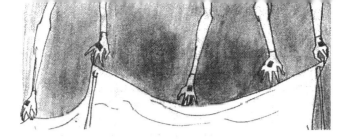

this wild country of the United States. It is found in the network of
anarchists, eco-activists, and cooperative farmers in North Central
Wisconsin who are stopping a new centralized electrical scheme that
would destroy pristine wilderness, steal fields from family farms, and
run up costs for basic utilities. It inspires dozens of pirate radio stations refusing to submit to the new FCC regulations and swapping
their regional recordings online to fill the airwaves with as many
voices as possible, from San Diego to Maine. It is also found in the
free yellow bike project in Portland, Oregon set up by a handful of
bike enthusiast friends with some repair skills and a connection at the
local junkyard. The Yellow Bike Project, replicated in many cities, simply allows yellow bikes to be available to the public for free, park-
ing them unlocked anywhere in the city. Folk anarchy also connects
the dedicated web of strangers and coconspirators stretched from
Austin to Gainesville who are providing shelter for runaway teens
escaping abusive situations. Folk anarchy can even be found in the
oppressive environments of schools and workplaces. Folk anarchy is
on the edges of favelas and shantytowns, it is in the hearts of people
yelling "Homes Not jails!" and then actually doing something about

it. It can be uncovered in trainyards and on aircraft carriers. Folk anarchy tonight sings songs in jails and tells stories in homeless shelters. Folk anarchy is dancing at the next Against Me! concert, it will keep you awake while scamming copies at your overnight copyshop job. It is what other people are doing and maybe folk anarchy is what you have been doing for weeks, or decades, independent of this book and its interpretations. Folk anarchy unfolds in amazing ways. Folk anarchy can help us rethink not only our oppressions, but also our resistance.

Folk anarchy helps us find allies and construct plans regardless of our size or how outlandish our dreams are. Folk anarchy allows us to break down the obstacles that disrupt our best efforts. Folk anarchy gives us an evolving language to explain the things we feel, defend what we do and explain it to others. It allows us to identify dinosaur thought, to point out the dangers of efficiency and experts, to express the hidden possibilities of chaos and communal heroism. It gives voice to what our heart already knows. Folk anarchy provides a much needed challenge to the dinosaurs. It can be so ordinary as to be missed by their surveillance cameras and clever enough to befuddle their intelligence units. It can slip past their sentries, it can swarm, pulse, and overwhelm. Sometimes it can help us disappear unpredictably. It can be today's news or it can be drawn from history. It works its magic in streets, infoshops, and around kitchen tables.

You can use folk anarchy to seek out allies in unlikely places. It can move computers to Chiapas. Folk anarchy can help you avoid burnout and resentment. It offers perspective and provides a way to organize. You can do folk anarchy in every project that stirs your imagination and with anyone that seeks to end hierarchies based on power. You can use the lessons of folk anarchy to see through the manipulations of others and to avoid the pitfalls that sap your resources and morale. It can help you create a book and distribute it to hundreds of friends you haven't yet met. Folk anarchy is a process, a way to organize and perceive. It doesn't seek to add or subtract from anarchy, but highlight its most enduring and successful characteristics: decentralization, mutual aid, doing-it-yourself, voluntary association, and chaos. We do all of these positive things, while accepting the tedious task of deconstructing the rhetorical techniques of folks (whether they call themselves "anarchists" or not) who embrace the tactics of dinosaurs and wish to water down our own efforts.

Folk anarchy is creating our own choices. It is an exploding bomb of possibilities, a rejection of everything embodied by the State and the boss, the bully and the banker, the abusive husband and the cop. It is a name, however arbitrary, for an infinite multitude of actions taken to erode the constraints of authority freeing ourselves from dependence on the ravages of capitalism and the murderous intrigues of the State. It's what opens up our time to work with and support others in their struggles for similar goals. It's what gets us up in the morning without coffee or an alarm clock. Folk anarchy is what gives us hope when we've lost everything, providing the music to the movement of the stars on the last sunset the world of the dinosaurs will ever see.

Friends, this is folk anarchy.

A Letter From Geneva

Anarchy didn't die with the end of the Spanish Civil War. It lived on and reappeared as soon as the dinosaurs averted their eyes. Revolutions such as ours are not a once-in-a-lifetime affair. No, they are as perpetual as the changing of the seasons. I hope you realize that this book is a love letter—a love letter to all of you beautiful anarchists, and to the new lives you are all creating. In a world without hope, you gave us hope. In a time of terror, you taught us to love. In a world without a future you gave us the greatest gift possible—the present.

The process of writing this book has been as dangerous as its content: pages smuggled across international borders, emails sent from Indymedia Centers in the middle of anti-G8 riots, draft corrections made in villages in Chiapas and squats in New York City, and art drawn during long rides in boxcars crisscrossing the Great Plains of North America. We hope this is a new type of book, not one written by academics or the latest media-darlings, but by people on the street, just like you. If you are an accountant, economist, king, officer, taxonomist, or any other type of dinosaur: Consider this your final warning. However; if you find even the smallest light of inspiration in these words—all of you out there, whether you choose to call yourself an anarchist or not, this book is for you.

This book is for you: for everything you've done and for everything you're going to do. We hope you find it useful. If there is a great secret in this world, it is that you are invincible. We would like you to realize your own abilities and to utilize the gifts which you have been blessed with. There are thousands like you out there, anarchists one and all. There is no secret for revolution, no grand dialectic, no master theory. Revolution is simple. Go out and meet folks who are just as passionate as you are—and if they don't realize it, help them along the way. Combine forces, scheme, and make plans. Then, *do it*. The power of the dinosaurs will eventually collapse like the house of tattered cards that it is. The ability of (extra)ordinary people to take control of their own lives shines forth even now, ever-growing, ever-changing, and ever dear to our hearts.

No more fond farewells, no more rousing conclusions, or elegies for yesterday. These pages have offered a glimpse into this world of everyday miracles that we like to call "folk anarchy"… or just "anarchy" when it suits us. Let us part with a grin, a conspiratorial wink, a warm embrace, and the lightest of kisses upon your cheek. We will cross paths again, we assure you of that.

This is the end of our little book, but today is just the beginning for anarchy.